*We dedicate this book to our
colleagues Edward S. Rosenbluh, Ph.D.
(1937–2000), and W. Rodney Fowler, Ed.D.,
pioneers in the field of Crisis Management.
Over the years we have taught alongside
them, and we continue to learn from them.*

About the Authors

DR. JAMES L. GREENSTONE

Dr. James L. Greenstone is a police psychologist and the director of the Psychological Services Unit of the Fort Worth Police Department. He supervises the Department's Peer Support Team, is the coordinator of the Critical Incident Stress Management Program, and is a member of the department's Hostage and Crisis Negotiation Team. He has been in practice for 35 years and has been a police officer for 22 years. He is certified as a Master Peace Officer and as a Mental Health Peace Officer by the Texas Commission on Law Enforcement Officer Standards and Education. He is a member of the Graduate Criminal Justice Faculty of Walden University and the Graduate Psychology Faculty of Capella University. Formerly, he was an adjunct professor of law at the Texas Wesleyan University School of Law and was Lead Hostage and Crisis Negotiations instructor at the North Central Texas Council of Governments Regional Police Academy. He is a licensed professional counselor, a licensed marriage and family therapist, and a dispute mediator and arbitrator. He holds earned degrees in Clinical Psychology, Education, Criminal Justice, and Law. He interned at the Devereux Foundation in Devon, Pennsylvania.

Dr. Greenstone is a member of the Crisis Intervention Advisory Board for the City of Fort Worth, Texas, and was appointed by the mayor of Fort Worth to the City/County Mental Health Task Force. He is the editor-in-chief of the *Journal of Police Crisis Negotiations,* an international journal published by Haworth Publishing, Inc. Previously, he was the editor-in-chief of *Emotional First Aid: A Journal of Crisis Intervention.*

Dr. Greenstone is the chair of the American Board of Examiners in Crisis Intervention* and a diplomate in Crisis Intervention, a diplomate in Police Psychology from the Society for Police and Criminal

*American Board of Examiners in Crisis Intervention: *www.emotionalfirstaid.com*

Psychology, a diplomate in Psychology and Medicine from the American Board of Forensic Examiners, a diplomate in Traumatic Stress from the American Academy of Experts in Traumatic Stress, and a fellow of the College of the American College of Forensic Examiners. He is a practitioner member of the Academy of Family Mediators.

DR. SHARON C. LEVITON

Dr. Sharon C. Leviton holds degrees in Education and Crisis Intervention, and is a crisis specialist and a family dispute mediator in private practice in Fort Worth, Texas. Formerly, she was an adjunct professor of law at the Texas Wesleyan University School of Law, and an individual and family psychotherapist in private practice.

Dr. Leviton is the vice-chair of the American Board of Examiners in Crisis Intervention and a diplomate in Crisis Intervention, a diplomate of the International Academy of Behavioral Medicine Counseling and Psychotherapy, Inc., a practitioner member of the Academy of Family Mediators, and a member of the American Red Cross Disaster Mental Health Team.

Dr. Leviton is an editor of the *Journal of Police Crisis Negotiations*. She has authored books, articles, papers, and editorials in the fields of psychotherapy, Crisis Intervention, stress management, and dispute resolution. She was appointed by the Fort Worth City Council to the Disciplinary Appeals Board.

Brief Contents

Contents

In addition to listing the areas covered in the chapters, this table of contents is a step-by-step guide to the intervention process and should be used by interveners to guide an intervention in an orderly fashion.

- Know what a crisis is.
- Use the crisis cube to plot the course of a crisis.
- Differentiate between the need for Crisis Intervention and the need for counseling.
- Determine whether the sufferer fits the profile of a crisis-prone person.
- Isolate the events that precipitated the crisis.
- Determine whether the sufferer is in crisis.
- Know the emotional, cognitive, and behavioral signs and symptoms of psychological reactions to crisis.

- Act immediately.
- Take control.
   Be clear about what and whom you are attempting to control.
   Enter the crisis scene cautiously.
   Appear stable, supportive, and able to establish structure.
   Be clear in your introductory statements.
   Do not promise things that might not happen.
   Direct and arrange the pattern of standing or sitting.

They might be used before, during, or after an intervention. The intervener might decide not to use them.

- Understand the designation and role of lead teams and lead interveners.
- Clarify the division of responsibility of team members.
- Be familiar with the positioning of team members.
- Be prepared to accept personal responsibility as a team member.
- As a team, apply the procedure for effective Crisis Intervention.
- Some Mistaken Assumptions:
  "If you can't help them, at least don't hurt them."
  "I know exactly how you feel."
  "If I ask about suicide, the person might do it."
  "I can relax after the parties are seated."
  "Listening to and acknowledging feelings implies agreement."
  "My degree, badge, or profession will automatically make me an effective intervener."

CHAPTER 5

SPECIAL ISSUES   47

- Take safety seriously.
  Approach the crisis slowly.
  Don't park in front of the building where the crisis is occurring.
  Approach doors carefully.
  Expect the unexpected.
  Listen for clues.
  Maintain control.
  Visually frisk the people involved.
  Remain observant.
  Separate disputants if necessary.
  Seat the victims.
  Sit attentively.
  Do not turn your back.
  Bring disputants back together.
  Maintain eye contact with your partner.
  Break eye contact between disputants.
  Plan your office with safety in mind.
  Intervene with a partner.
  Play the "what if" game.
  Make contingency plans.
- Be sensitive to gender, racial, and ethnic issues.
  Become aware of your own cultural biases.
  Ask for clarification as needed.
  Do not impose your personal values.
  Be willing to test, adapt, and change your perceptions to fit your new experience with people from another culture.
- Be able to identify students at risk for violent behavior.
- Be able to identify adults at risk for violent behavior.

CHAPTER 6

INTERVENER SURVIVAL   57

- Recognize the signs and symptoms of stress and burnout.
- Take care of yourself:
    Eat nutritiously.
    Get enough rest.
    Exercise regularly.
    Set realistic goals for yourself.
    Plan for fun and relaxation.
    Be responsible for self-direction.
    Be concerned about personal safety.
- Become aware of your own personal issues.
- Be aware of Critical Incident Stress Management.

CHAPTER 7

CHILDREN'S REACTIONS TO CRISIS   67

- Teachers: Take care of yourself and each other.
- Learn the "typical" reactions of normal children in each age group.
- Refer the family for professional help as needed.
- Create age- and grade-appropriate activities for children in crisis.
    Preschool
    Elementary School
    Junior and Senior High School
        Journalism
        Science
        English Composition
        Literature
        Psychology
        Peer Counseling
        Health
        Art
        Speech and Drama
        Mathematics
        Civics and Government
        History

CHAPTER 8

HOT-LINE WORKERS   80

- Learn the Do's to effective hot-line interactions.
- Avoid the Don'ts that can lead to ineffective hot-line interactions.
- Learn to handle the difficult caller.

CHAPTER 9

FAMILY CRISIS   84

- Follow the 30 steps for handling family crisis.
- Learn how parents can help their children cope with crisis-related feelings.
- In preparing for holidays, follow the 20 steps for avoiding holiday crisis.

CHAPTER 10

GRIEF   90

- Look for the grief component in the crisis.
- Recognize what grief victims might experience.
- Teach the sufferer to use self-intervention.
- Help the sufferer cope with separation or loss.
- Recognize the recurring reactions of sufferers of tragic events.

CHAPTER 11

LEGAL IMPLICATIONS OF CRISIS INTERVENTION   99

- Know the laws that govern what you do.
- Treat victims as human beings rather than as cases.
- Intervene within the limits of your background, training, and experience.
- If you begin an intervention, stay with it unless you are relieved by someone with greater skill.
- If possible, obtain consent before intervening.
- Maintain confidentiality of all information you obtain.
- Document all your actions in an intervention.
- Maintain your professional competency.
- Respect the victim's right to privacy.
- Think before you act.

Preface

The Elements of Crisis Intervention is intended for the following groups of people:

Crisis workers
Hot-line workers
Parents
Teachers
Counselors and psycho-
  therapists
Support group members and
  leaders
Outreach groups
Police officers
Probation and parole officers
Peer counselors
Teenage support groups
Attorneys
Emergency medical service
  personnel
Fire fighters
Bartenders

School-based crisis manage-
  ment team members
Social workers
School violence counselors
School crisis response team
  members
Hostage negotiators
First response personnel
Clergy
Flight attendants
Judiciary
Government agency personnel
Mediators
Nurses
Secondary victims
First responders
Receptionists

We have reduced the practice of Crisis Intervention to its basic elements so they can be applied as broadly as possible, and we present them in a format that is useful both for the experienced professional and for the novice. We know of no other text that approaches the subject so directly. We have spent much time in our careers eliminating confusion about procedures and about the relationship between Crisis Intervention and other behavioral sciences. This book reinforces the theoretical framework that postulates Crisis Intervention as a viable discipline in itself.

Because this is a practical guide, most theory has been purposely omitted. We suggest that *Elements of Crisis Intervention* be used as a supplement in classes in psychology, counseling, psychotherapy, crisis intervention, crisis counseling, health services, emergency medicine, police science, negotiations, school-based crisis management plans, and in other related practical and applied courses at all levels. It is also appropriate for training courses in Crisis Intervention and Crisis Counseling. The experienced intervener can use the book independently, in the classroom, in the office, and in the field.

HOW TO USE THIS BOOK

This book is designed to aid in practical, day-to-day, on-the-scene Crisis Intervention. In addition to listing the areas covered in the chapters, the table of contents is a step-by-step guide to the intervention process and should be used by interveners to guide an intervention in an orderly fashion. For the experienced crisis intervener, the table of contents is a helpful reminder of the steps to be taken during an intervention. Novices may need to read the entire book carefully before they can use the table of contents effectively, and they should understand that the full value of this book depends on their gaining theoretical depth and practical training.

Interveners can also look up material according to the activity they want to perform or by the intervener's role (for example, police officer or therapist). These listings are printed on the inside front and back covers of the book.

THE ELEMENTS OF CRISIS INTERVENTION

A crisis occurs when unusual stress temporarily renders an individual unable to direct life effectively. As the stress mounts and the usual coping mechanisms provide neither relief nor remedy, the person often experiences extreme feelings of fear, anger, grief, hostility, helplessness, hopelessness, and alienation from self, family, and society. Stress can be a reaction to a single event or to several events occurring simultaneously or serially.

Ordinary upsets can be handled with day-to-day skills. Crises happen suddenly and unexpectedly and seem arbitrary. Inexplicable events raise stress to a critical level. Crisis Intervention is a timely and skillful intrusion into a personal crisis to defuse a potentially disastrous situation before physical or emotional destruction occurs. The intervener attempts to return the sufferer to a level of precrisis functioning at a time when his or her life lacks structure. Rosenbluh (1975) calls this "emotional first aid." Just as people bleed physically, they can also bleed—and bleed to death—emotionally. Crisis Intervention is not therapy. It is the skilled attempt to stop the emotional bleeding in a way that will allow the individual to continue life effectively. The intervener makes quick, accurate, critical decisions about the victim and mobilizes needed resources. Successful Crisis Intervention achieves problem management, not problem resolution. The intervener who has helped the victim of a crisis regain precrisis stability has met the goals of Crisis Intervention. Although an individual may require support after a crisis that can include psychotherapy or counseling, effective Crisis Intervention can significantly reduce the need for intensive treatment.

To a great extent, we apply the theory that "A crisis is a crisis is a crisis" (Leviton, 1982, p. 10). Although one can certainly argue that a particular incident requires a specific response, that incident-specific response is always grounded in the basic Crisis Intervention theory and procedures that are the subject of this book. As Rosenbluh puts it, "If we are to be helpful, we must remain effective" (1975), and the keys to effectiveness are having a clear understanding of the elements of Crisis Intervention and the ability to apply them practically. A return to the basics is nearly always beneficial, and is continually instructive, to all who labor in the vineyard of crisis management.

We would like to thank Suzanne Raif, David Leviton, Julie Martinez, Sara Dovre Wudali, Kim Svetich-Will, and Robin Gold for their invaluable assistance. We would also like to thank the following reviewers: Dr. Dee Barclift, Jacksonville State University; Dr. Fernando Cordero, Alan Hancock College; Dr. Lyn Harris, Jamestown Community College; Dr. Marianne Piet, Aurora University; Dr. James Robinson, San Bernadino Valley College; and Dr. Alice Yick Flannigan, Research Insights.

James L. Greenstone
Sharon C. Leviton

APPROACH TO CRISIS INTERVENTION

WHAT IS A CRISIS?

Crisis results from stress and tension in a person's life. Stress is the key element in crisis development. As stress mounts to unusual proportions and the individual's coping skills become increasingly ineffective, the potential for crisis occurs. The *crisis cube* is a three-dimensional representation of crisis development (see Figure 1.1). The crisis cube illustrates how, before a crisis, the normal level of functioning can be interrupted by the occurrence of unusual stress caused by single, multiple, or serial factors. When this happens, a person attempts to solve problems and handle tension in usual ways. As this fails, a downward spiral of ineffective behavior, referred to as *maladaptive behavior*, occurs. Crisis Intervention is the act of interrupting the downward spiral as skillfully and as quickly as possible and, in so doing, of returning the victim to a precrisis level of coping. As the time line on the crisis cube indicates, every moment is crucial to the intervener. The longer the line of maladaptive behavior goes unchallenged and uninterrupted, the greater is the possibility of increased personality disintegration and increased need for psychological treatment or therapy after the crisis is over. The intervener's skill and the timeliness of the intervention can determine the possibility of the victim's later functioning and growth.

Crisis Intervention (or Crisis Management) and counseling (or psychotherapy) must be separated by function and application. Crisis Intervention/Management is an attempt to deal quickly with an immediate problem. Often it requires providing for victims that which the victims cannot provide for themselves. This can include a physical or

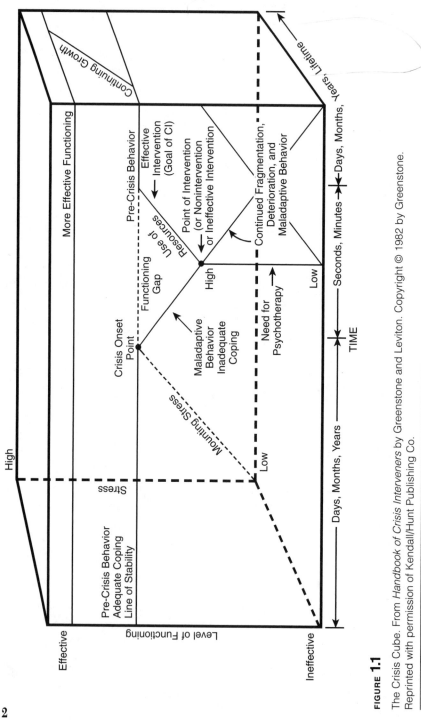

FIGURE 1.1

The Crisis Cube. From *Handbook of Crisis Interveners* by Greenstone and Leviton. Copyright © 1982 by Greenstone. Reprinted with permission of Kendall/Hunt Publishing Co.

2

emotional crutch to lean on and even direction by the intervener at a time in the victim's life when self-direction may be impossible. Crisis Intervention is to emergency-room medicine what a medical practice is to a psychotherapy practice. Psychotherapy and Crisis Intervention must never be confused. To do so could deny victims what they need at a very critical time in their lives. To be sure, every therapist will bene- fit from developing Crisis Intervention skills, but to assume that Crisis Intervention and counseling are the same is courting disaster (see Corsini, 1981).

Psychotherapy, crisis counseling, short-term psychotherapy, or other forms of therapeutic intervention may be appropriate after Crisis Intervention. Interveners should make no assumptions about helping the victim find solutions to the problems that precipitated the crisis. Management, not resolution, is the intervener's goal, and at best this goal is a very short term one. If the victim needs care after intervention, referral for appropriate short- or long-term therapeutic involvement is the additional responsibility of the intervener. Rosenbluh (1981) refers to Crisis Intervention as "emotional first aid." Crisis Intervention is the emotional equivalent of physical first aid and must be applied in the same skillful and timely fashion to allow victims to maximize their involvement in psychotherapy or counseling if required.

The following are indicators of a person who may be prone to cri- sis. We also present a list of precipitating factors. Finally, signs and symptoms of a person in crisis are presented as a guide to recognition of and need for intervention. These events must be understood from the sufferers' perspectives of what a crisis is for them.

INDICATORS THAT CAN CHARACTERIZE A CRISIS-PRONE PERSON

- Alienation from lasting and meaningful personal relationships
- Inability to use life support systems such as family, friends, and social groups
- Difficulty in learning from experience; the individual continues to make the same mistakes
- A history of previously experienced crises that have not been effectively resolved
- A history of mental disorder or severe emotional imbalance
- Feelings of low self-esteem

- Provocative, impulsive behavior resulting from unresolved inner conflict
- A history of poor marital relationships
- Excessive use of drugs, including alcohol abuse
- Marginal income
- Lack of regular, fulfilling work
- Unusual or frequent physical injuries
- Frequent changes in residence
- Frequent encounters with the law

EVENTS THAT CAN PRECIPITATE A CRISIS

- An accident in the home
- An automobile accident, with or without injury
- Being arrested; appearing in court
- Changes in job situation and income involving either promotion or demotion
- Change in school status
- Death of a significant person in one's life
- Divorce or separation
- A delinquency episode either in childhood or adulthood (in childhood, skipping school or running away from home; in adulthood, failure to pay debts)
- Entry into school
- Abortion or out-of-wedlock pregnancy
- Physical illness
- Acute episodes of mental disorder
- Retirement
- Natural disasters or man-made disasters
- Sexual difficulties
- Major change in living conditions
- Gaining a new family member (for example, through birth, adoption, or parents or adult children moving in)
- Dealing with a blended family
- Foreclosure on a mortgage or loan
- Actual or impending loss of something significant in one's life

Although a particular stressful situation might not induce crisis, a combination of several such *stressful* events could push the individual to the crisis point.

RECOGNIZING A PERSON IN CRISIS

1. Recognition depends on
   a. The intervener's awareness of what the victim is communicating verbally and nonverbally
   b. The intervener's sensing capabilities
2. Different people indicate crisis in different ways:
   a. Crying out, exploding, verbalizing
   b. Withdrawal, depression, or both
3. If possible, the intervener should obtain information from family and friends about the victim's precrisis behavior and note disruptions in previous behavior and modes of ineffective functioning.
4. Profile of a person in crisis:
   a. Bewilderment: "I never felt this way before."
   b. Danger: "I am so nervous and scared."
   c. Confusion: "I can't think clearly."
   d. Impasse: "I feel stuck; nothing I do helps."
   e. Desperation: "I've got to do something."
   f. Apathy: "Nothing can help me."
   g. Helplessness: "I can't take care of myself."
   h. Urgency: "I need help now!!!"
   i. Discomfort: "I feel miserable, restless, and unsettled."
   j. Numbness: "I don't feel anything . . . anything. It's all surreal."

At this point, the victim is not totally in control of his or her life and feels the panic resulting from this realization. Victims may flail about emotionally, verbally, or even physically as they experience this lack of control.

COMMON SIGNS AND SYMPTOMS OF PSYCHOLOGICAL REACTIONS TO CRISIS

Emotional

Anticipatory anxiety	Uncertainty
Generalized anxiety	Fear
Shock	Helplessness
Denial	Depression
Insecurity	Panic
Fatigue	Despair

Survivor guilt
Feeling out of control
Grief
Outrage
Numbness

Frustration
Inadequacy
Feeling overwhelmed
Anger
Irritability

Cognitive

Confusion
Poor attention span
Poor concentration
Flashbacks

Loss of trust
Difficulties in decision making
Nightmares

Behavioral

Withdrawal
Sleep disturbances
Angry outbursts
Change in activity
Change in appetite
Increased fatigue
Excessive use of sick leave
Alcohol or drug abuse
Difficulty functioning at
    normal ability level
Antisocial acts
Frequent visits to physician
    for nonspecific complaints

Anger at God
Loss of desire to attend
    religious services
Regression
Crying
Change in communications
Preoccupation with the crisis to
    the exclusion of other areas
    of life
Diminished job performance
Unresponsiveness
Hysterical reactions
Irritability

Procedures for Effective Crisis Intervention

The Need for an Established Procedure

Crisis interveners learn early in their careers that having an established procedure to follow is vital to their effectiveness. An intervention is a logical and orderly process. Step-by-step the intervener assists the sufferer in moving from a state of disequilibrium to at least his or her pre-crisis level of functioning.

The time to develop a procedure is before attempting to intervene. Every action and every interaction must be thoughtful, measured, and purposeful. This is not a time to say "I'll try this out and see what happens." Such a haphazard approach would court disaster for the victim and intervener.

Crisis situations can and do occur at inconvenient and odd times of the day, night, weekend or holidays. When the phone rings in the middle of the night and the voice on the other end says "I'm going to kill myself," the prepared intervener will automatically access his or her proven plan of response. Having the ability to mentally run through a checklist provides the comfort of knowing that all the steps were covered.

We have used the following Crisis Intervention model for the past 30 years. We offer it for your consideration.

Crisis Intervention consists of six major components (see Figure 2.1):

I. IMMEDIACY	IV. DISPOSITION
II. CONTROL	V. REFERRAL
III. ASSESSMENT	VI. FOLLOW-UP

Immediacy

Control

Assessment

Disposition

Referral

Follow-up

FIGURE **2.1**

Crisis Intervention procedure

The following outlines describe effective Crisis Intervention procedures.

I. *Act immediately to stop the emotional bleeding.*

Intervention begins at the moment the intervener encounters the person in crisis. The intervener must immediately attempt to

- Relieve anxiety
- Prevent further disorientation
- Ensure that sufferers do not harm themselves or cause harm to others

II. *Take control.*

a. Be clear about what and whom you are attempting to control.

The purpose of assuming control is not to conquer or overwhelm the victim. Rather, it is to help reorder the chaos that exists in the sufferer's world at the moment of crisis. The intervener provides the needed structure until the victim can regain control.

   b. Enter the crisis scene cautiously.

Approach any crisis situation slowly and carefully. Caution at this point can prevent unnecessary grief. Take a moment to mentally compute what you

- Hear
- See
- Smell
- Feel
- Sense
- Touch

   c. Appear stable, supportive, and able to establish structure.

Use your personal presence. Your strength, control, and calm in the crisis situation may exert the control the victim needs.

   d. Be clear in your introductory statements. The opening questions, directions, and other information you give the victim will often assist in gaining and in maintaining control.

INTERVENER: *Hello, I'm Sharon Leviton from the Crisis Center. Are you Mrs. Jones?*
MRS. JONES: *Yes. I don't know what you or anybody else can do. I just know . . . I can't stand it anymore.*
INTERVENER: *I'd like to listen to what's bothering you. May I come in?*

   e. Do not promise things that might not happen. For example, don't say, "I can fix it. Everything will be all right." It might not be!
   f. Direct and arrange the pattern of standing and sitting to gain the victim's attention.
   g. Guide the sufferer with your eyes and voice rather than through physical force.
   h. Use physical force only as a last resort, and only if you are trained and authorized to use it.

i. Remove the victim from the crisis situation if possible. Otherwise, remove the crisis from the victim.
j. Be creative in taking control.
k. Break eye contact between disputants.
l. Separate the victims if necessary.

Specific ways of gaining control in a crisis situation vary, depending on the skills and abilities of the intervener. The task allows wide latitude for creativity. Possible ways of taking control include the following:

- Creating a loud noise to gain attention.
- Speaking in a quieter tone than the victim is.
- Breaking eye contact between two disputants to reduce tension.
- Making an odd request: "May I see that book over there?"

Victims will respond to structure and to those who represent it if they sense it is genuine and not just a technique.

III. Assess the situation.

- What is troubling the victim now?
- Why did the person go into crisis at this particular time?
- Which problem among those that might be present is of immediate concern?
- Which problem must be dealt with before other problems can be handled?
- Which problem among those presented can be immediately managed?
- What variables will hinder the problem-management process?
- How can the intervener implement the most effective help in the least time?

To accomplish an effective assessment, do the following:

a. Evaluate on the spot. Don't wait.
b. Make the evaluation quick, accurate, and comprehensive enough to give a total picture.
c. Do not take a lengthy life history. Focus your assessment on the present crisis and the events that occurred within the last 48 hours. What were the precipitating events?

INTERVENER: *Tell me what happened in the last few days.*
MARY: *I lost my job today.*

INTERVENER: *Your job was important to you.*
MARY: *Yes. I have to have it because my husband walked out on me yesterday.*
INTERVENER: *You seem very frightened.*
MARY: *I'm scared to death. My husband left me. I've got three little babies. My mom is dying of cancer, and I don't have a job. We're three months behind in the rent. I've got nowhere to turn. There's no way I'm going to make it. I've got nowhere to go, so I may as well end it. My kids would be better off . . .*

d. Ask short, direct questions.

INTERVENER: *How are you feeling, John?*
JOHN: *I feel lost and strange.*
INTERVENER: *What do you mean by "strange"?*
JOHN: *I can't explain it.*
INTERVENER: *Can you put another feeling with strange?*
JOHN: *Hopeless. I can't find any way to cope with Judy's death.*

e. Ask questions one at a time.
f. Allow the victim enough time to answer your questions.

INTERVENER: *Did you ever feel this way before?*
(Pause)
JOHN: *I can't think too clearly. That's what is so scary to me.*
INTERVENER: *Take your time, John. We're in no rush.*

g. Do not increase victims' confusion by bombarding them with many questions at once.
h. Learn to accept discomfort with silence. Recognize the usefulness of silence in the intervention process.
i. Interrupt the victim judiciously. You can use periodic interruptions to clarify, to check the accuracy and your understanding of the victim's statements, and simply to remind the victim of your interest in the problem. Interrupt no more often than absolutely necessary.
j. Clarify the crisis. To be effective you must know what the crisis is.

INTERVENER: *Your fear of your dad finding out about your pregnancy seems to be causing your feelings of terror.*

ANN: *That's most of it. I disappointed and embarrassed him. He'll abandon me. He'll slap my mom around and blame her. I ruined it for everybody! I've got to run away.*

k. Allow the crisis to be the victim's crisis.

Avoid judgments, preachments, and putdowns. Don't belittle the victim or the crisis; crisis is always in the eye of the beholder. The way the victim currently perceives the world is the victim's reality. For example, don't say, "You're silly to be so worried. He wasn't worth it anyway. I know you'll find someone else next week."

l. Assess both the actual and the symbolic meaning of the crisis event. Remember that perception triggers crisis much more often than do facts.

m. Use the sufferer's body language and nonverbal behavior as a source of information. If you observe that the words and behavior do not match, question the discrepancy.

n. Listen for what is *not* being said. Attend to what the victim says and does. Be aware of what the victim has not done and what would normally be expected under current circumstances.

o. Recognize that your personal attributes contribute to your overall effectiveness.

- Remain reassuring and calm.
- Remain empathic and attentive.
- Remain supportive.
- Be willing to reach out to the sufferer, both physically and emotionally, as needed.
- Maintain a caring attitude that conveys a willingness to listen.

p. Allow the victim to speak freely and to ventilate feelings.

q. Help the victim to see the crisis as temporary rather than chronic.

r. In a multiple-victim situation (such as a family dispute), allow each person to speak without interruption by the other people involved. Establish ground rules immediately, and insist they be followed.

INTERVENER: *Mr. Jones, will you agree to listen while your wife talks to us?*

MR. JONES: *But she never shuts up.*
INTERVENER: *I will ensure that each of you has enough time to say what you need to. I'm very interested in hearing both of you.*
MR. JONES: *OK, I'll agree to that. But she better be careful. You have to watch her.*
INTERVENER: *Mrs. Jones, will you agree to listen while Mr. Jones talks?*
MRS. JONES: *Oh, yes. You can count on me.*

    s. Return control to the victim as soon as possible.

IV. Decide how to handle the situation after you have assessed it.

Heightened stress closes down options and generally produces "tunnel vision" in the victim. When effective intervention occurs, the victim becomes more receptive to

- Exploring options
- Thinking creatively
- Solving problems

    a. Help the victim identify and mobilize personal resources.

INTERVENER: *Mrs. Smith, what is one way that you might manage that trapped feeling when John is out of town?*
MRS. SMITH: *I can call the lady next door and trade babysitting with her.*
INTERVENER: *Would you feel comfortable with that?*
MRS. SMITH: *She's very caring and responsible, and it could be good for the kids and for me. I wouldn't get so angry and upset with the kids. I can't believe what I almost did.*
INTERVENER: *Do you have any other ideas?*
MRS. SMITH: *John and I need some professional help about a few things. Could you help me find a family counselor? I'm ready to get on with this.*
INTERVENER: *Yes, I can.*

    b. Mobilize social resources.
    c. Hold out hope that solutions are possible.
    d. Develop options.
    e. Help the parties to the crisis make an agreement.

Almost any agreement answers the following questions:

Who?
What?
Where?
When?
Why?
What if?
How much?

MR. JONES: *I'll baby-sit on Tuesday evenings so Mary can take care of her dad.*
INTERVENER: *What time on Tuesday?*
MR. JONES: *I can get home by 5:00 P.M. Remember, I can't keep this up after January.*
INTERVENER: *So, after January, Mary will have to make other plans about the visitation.*
MRS. JONES: *I understand. The pressure should be over by then.*
INTERVENER: *What if you can't baby-sit on Tuesday at that time?*
MR. JONES: *I'll be responsible for making other arrangements.*

V. *Refer as needed. Follow up if possible or as agreed.*

a. Investigate possible referral sources by checking local telephone directories and manuals that list specialized services.
b. Check with professionals such as doctors, lawyers, and clergy in the community. Determine if they take referrals from crisis situations; not all do. Ask if they would be on call to assist if needed.
c. Contact local hospital emergency care units and get to know the staff. Find out about requirements for admission and treatment.
d. Visit agencies in the community that provide assistance to crisis victims. Find out if they are willing and equipped to accept referrals and if they will
    (1) give a crisis-victim referral high priority in scheduling,
    (2) understand the need for proper crisis referrals, and
    (3) give feedback when an intervener tries to follow up with someone who has been referred.

e. Determine the hours of operation of each potential referral agency. Are the agencies staffed by people or answering machines?

f. Make a list of acceptable referral sources.

g. Be sure the phone numbers, addresses, and names of contact persons are current.

h. Determine what state and national referral agencies or hot lines crisis victims can access.

i. Update your referral list regularly. Add reliable agencies once you have checked them. Eliminate unreliable agencies as your experience with each dictates. Delete agencies that no longer provide the needed crisis services.

j. Determine the required fees for services and acceptable methods of payment.

k. Determine which agencies will accept referrals of crisis victims with limited financial resources.

l. Know the availability of transportation to and from the referral source. Sometimes the lack of this information will cause the referral process to break down even though other aspects of the intervention have been properly conducted.

m. Find out if the offices of the referral source have made provisions for persons with physical disabilities.

n. Have your list of referral sources available for use during an intervention.

o. When you are making a referral, do the following:

   (1) Print the information about the referral source on a card or piece of paper for the victim.

   (2) Carefully review the information with the victim.

   (3) In a telephone intervention, give the referral information slowly, clearly, and concisely. Ask the victim to repeat the information you have given and to write down the information if possible.

   (4) If you feel it might be helpful, help the victim make contact with the referral agency. For example, place the call to the agency from your office.

   (5) Double-check the accuracy of the referral information you provide to the victim or the family.

   (6) Ask the victim if the information is clear and understandable.

(7) Ask victims if they know of any circumstance that would prevent their making contact with the referral agency or keeping an appointment with the agency.

(8) If problems are identified, attempt to deal with them on the spot.

VI. Follow up with victims to ensure that they made contact with the referral agency.

a. If the victim has not made contact with the referral agency within a reasonable amount of time, try to find out why.

b. If necessary, attempt to help victims deal with their reasons for not contacting the referral agency.

c. Re-refer victims as appropriate.

TWO USEFUL TOOLS TO AID IN ASSESSMENT

Tables 2.1 and 2.2 can help interveners with their assessments. We have found these useful tools in recognizing what is going on with an individual because they aid in our sensitivity to that person's situation.

The scales might be used before, during, or after an intervention. The intervener might decide not to use them.

The following are explanations for each category on the American Academy of Crisis Interveners Lethality Scale (Table 2.1) and the Life Change Index Scale (Table 2.2):

Age: Self-explanatory
Stress: At what level is the victim experiencing stress?
Resources: Personal, family, and social support available
Marital status: Self-explanatory
Psychological functioning: Person's functioning before this event
Symptoms: Self-explanatory
Communications: General level of interpersonal interaction
Physical condition: Self-explanatory
Suicide by close family member: History of suicide in immediate family
Depressed/agitated: Self-explanatory
Prior suicidal behavior: History of attempts

TABLE
2.1

AMERICAN ACADEMY OF CRISIS INTERVENERS LETHALITY SCALE

Date _____   **Criteria:** Minimal risk (0–15) _____
                                                 Low risk   (16–30) _____
Name _____   Medium risk   (31–46) _____
                                                 High risk   (47–60) _____

Circle response in appropriate row and column and place score from top column in extreme right column. Sum all scores and match total with criteria.

		0	1	2	3	4	Score
Age	Male	0–12		13–44	45–64	65+	
	Female	0–12	13–44	45+			
Stress		Low		Medium		High	
Resouces		Good	Fair		Poor		
Marital Status		Married with children	Married without children		Widowed, Single	Divorced	
Psychological Functioning		Stable			Unstable		
Symptoms (alcoholism, drug addiction, homo-sexuality)		Absent			Present		
Communications		Open			Blocked		
Physical Condition		Good	Fair			Poor	
Suicide by Close Family Member		No		Yes			
Depressed/ Agitated		No				Yes	
Prior Suicidal Behavior		No		Yes			
Reaction by Significant Others		Helpful			Not helpful		
Financial Stress		Absent		Present			
Suicidal Plan		None	Few details	Means selected		Highly specific plan	

(continued)

TABLE

2.1   **AMERICAN ACADEMY OF CRISIS INTERVENERS LETHALITY SCALE (CONTINUED)**

	0	1	2	3	4	Score
Occupation	Non-helping profession, Other occupation	M.D., Dentist, Attorney, Helping profession	Psychiatrist, Police officer, Unem- ployed			
Residence	Rural	Suburban	Urban			
Living Arrangements	With others				Alone	
Time of Year		Spring				
Day of Week		Sunday, Wednesday	Monday			
Serious Arguments with Spouse	No	Yes				
Loss of Significant Other (Recently)		Focus of disappoint- ment				

Intervener _____   Total _____

Reprinted with permission of A.A.C.I.

Reaction by significant others: Self-explanatory
Financial stress: Self-explanatory
Suicidal plan: Current plan and specificity
Occupation: Self-explanatory
Residence: Self-explanatory
Living arrangements: Self-explanatory
Time of year: Current time of year
Day of week: Day of week crisis is occurring
Serious arguments with spouse: Self-explanatory
Significant other: Someone close to the victim who has
     disappointed or been lost to the victim through death,
     desertion, or divorce

TABLE
2.2

LIFE CHANGE INDEX SCALE

Look over the events listed in the Life Change Index Scale. Place a check (√) in the space next to a given event if it has happened to you within the last twelve months.

1.	Death of a spouse	1.	_____	100
2.	Divorce	2.	_____	73
3.	Marital separation from mate	3.	_____	65
4.	Detention in jail or other institution	4.	_____	63
5.	Death of a close family member	5.	_____	63
6.	Major personal injury or illness	6.	_____	53
7.	Marriage	7.	_____	50
8.	Being fired at work	8.	_____	47
9.	Marital reconciliation	9.	_____	45
10.	Retirement from work	10.	_____	45
11.	Major change in the health or behavior of a family member	11.	_____	44
12.	Pregnancy	12.	_____	40
13.	Sexual difficulties	13.	_____	39
14.	Gaining a new family member (e.g., through birth, adoption, oldster moving in, etc.)	14.	_____	39
15.	Major business readjustment (e.g., merger, reorganization, bankruptcy, etc.)	15.	_____	38
16.	Major change in financial state (e.g., either a lot worse off or a lot better off than usual)	16.	_____	37
17.	Death of a close friend	17.	_____	36
18.	Changing to a different line of work	18.	_____	36
19.	Major change in the number of arguments with spouse (e.g., either a lot more or a lot less than usual regarding child-rearing, personal habits, etc.)	19.	_____	35
20.	Taking on a mortgage greater than $10,000 (e.g., purchasing a home, business, etc.)	20.	_____	31
21.	Foreclosure on a mortgage or loan	21.	_____	30
22.	Major change in responsibilities at work (e.g., promotion, demotion, lateral transfer)	22.	_____	29
23.	Son or daughter leaving home (e.g., marriage, attending college, etc.)	23.	_____	29
24.	In-law troubles	24.	_____	29
25.	Oustanding personal achievement	25.	_____	28
26.	Spouse beginning or ceasing work outside the home	26.	_____	26
27.	Beginning or ceasing formal schooling	27.	_____	26
28.	Major change in living conditions (e.g., building a new home, remodeling, deterioration of home or neighborhood)	28.	_____	25
29.	Revision of personal habits (dress, manners, associations, etc.)	29.	_____	24
30.	Troubles with the boss	30.	_____	23
31.	Major change in working hours or conditions	31.	_____	20
32.	Change in residence	32.	_____	20
33.	Change to a new school	33.	_____	20
34.	Major change in usual type and/or amount of recreation	34.	_____	19
35.	Major change in church activities (e.g., a lot more or less than usual)	35.	_____	19

(continued)

TABLE

2.2   **LIFE CHANGE INDEX SCALE** (CONTINUED)

36. Major change in social activities (e.g., clubs, dancing, movies, visiting, etc.)	36. _____	18
37. Taking on a mortgage or loan less than $10,000 (e.g., purchasing a car, TV, freezer, etc.)	37. _____	17
38. Major change in sleeping habits (a lot more or a lot less sleep or change in time of day when asleep)	38. _____	16
39. Major change in number of family get-togethers (e.g., a lot more or a lot less than usual)	39. _____	15
40. Major change in eating habits (a lot more or a lot less food intake, or very different meal hours or surroundings)	40. _____	15
41. Vacation	41. _____	13
42. Christmas	42. _____	12
43. Minor violations of the law (e.g., traffic tickets, jaywalking, disturbing the peace, etc.)	43. _____	11

Source: Reprinted from the *Journal of Psychosomatic Research, 11,* pp. 213–218, by Holmes and Rahe, "Social Readjustment Rating Scale," © 1967 by Pergamon Press, Ltd. with permission from Elsevier Science.

Scoring the Scale

Add the number of points next to each of your check marks. Place the total in the box below.

Total Life Change Units (LCU)

Interpreting Your Score

Dr. Thomas Holmes and his colleagues have clearly shown the relationship between recent life changes and future illness. The following are score categories and the associated probability of illness during the next two years for a person with that score:

0–150	No significant problem
150–199	Mild Life Crisis Level with a 35% chance of illness
200–299	Moderate Life Crisis Level with a 50% chance of illness
300 or over	Major Life Crisis Level with an 80% chance of illness

More than your *life change unit* (LCU) total score is related to your likelihood of illness. How you respond to changes and the amount of change are also important. Psychologists have found that when they match two groups, both with LCU totals higher than 300, those who developed physical illnesses had more difficulty in coping emotionally with life changes than did those who did not get sick. Aspects of how you go through your daily life, such as feeling the need to get everything done right on time, also are involved in how you handle potentially troublesome levels of life changes.

This means that after you total your LCUs, you also need to think about how emotionally strong you are to handle those changes and how good your present techniques are for relaxing and easing the pressure.

Your own LCU may suggest a higher—or lower—probability of illness depending on how you deal with stress as it arises. Just being aware of the concept of stress and how life changes increase stress can reduce your own likelihood of getting ill. You can reduce the stress of adjusting to change even further by developing specific techniques, such as relaxation, hobbies, exercise, and meditation.

About the Scale

The most common stress-producing situations in modern life involve fear and frustration. Most people would agree that there is a high degree of stress involved in negative events—such as death of a spouse, marital separation, or going to jail—related to these two emotions. But it took a group of researchers at the University of Washington School of Medicine to point out and quantify that *any* major life change, even a positive one, produces stress. The research team, led by Dr. Thomas Holmes, found in a group of 400 people a high relationship between their amount of life changes during the previous six months and their likelihood of getting sick.

Out of such research came the Life Change Index Scale, which rates 43 life events on the degree of stress each produces. The subsequent research needed to validate the scale is fascinating. The study mentioned earlier involved having 400 people count their LCU over a six-month and one-year period with the researcher then predicting, on the basis of LCU totals, which people would develop a major health problem during the next six months. Another study measured LCU totals in a group of 2,684 Navy and Marine personnel getting ready for a six-month cruise and predicted which people would need the most visits to sick bay during the cruise. Yet another research project involved predicting football injuries during a season on the basis of

LCU totals for team members before the season began. In each of these studies, plus numerous others, LCU totals were highly related to the likelihood of any specific person developing a major health problem.

As you look over the events, you will notice that an event such as marital separation produces more stress than does a personal illness or injury. But the positive change of getting back together, marital reconciliation, produces more stress than does a situation involving sex difficulties. Dr. Holmes and his colleagues were among the first researchers to quantify what stress expert Dr. Hans Selye had said for several years, that we must watch out for the impact of positive life changes as well as of those that are clearly negative. As Drs. Holmes and Masuda wrote, "If it takes too much effort to cope with the environment, we have less to spare for preventing disease. When life is too hectic and when coping attempts fail, illness is the unhappy result."

COMMUNICATING EFFECTIVELY WITH THOSE IN CRISIS

WHAT IS THE CRISIS?

Before a problem can be managed, the intervener must determine what the problem is. Often, more than one problem will be present in a situation. When this occurs, the following six questions may be asked to determine the priority for intervention.

1. Which problem is of most immediate concern?
2. Which problem would prove most damaging if not treated immediately?
3. Which problem can be most quickly resolved?
4. Which problem must be dealt with first before others can be handled?
5. What resources for handling problems are available?
6. What barriers and obstacles will hinder problem solving?[1]

Although it is necessary to answer all the preceding questions, if the intervener is to help manage the victim's crisis, the intervener must be able to acquire the needed information quickly and accurately. This means that the intervener must listen actively to the victim's total message and give the victim full concentration and undivided attention. Further, the intervener must sift through the person's words to gain information and insight into the victim's problems and views of those problems.

Every communication contains three messages: a content message, a feeling message, and a meaning message. The content message provides

---

[1] From *Emotional First Aid* by E. S. Rosenbluh. Copyright ©1981 by Rosenbluh. This and all other quotes from the same source are reprinted with permission. Dr. E. S. Rosenbluh.

information about what the sender believes, thinks, or perceives the situation to be. The feeling message conveys the nature and intensity of the sender's emotion about the situation. The meaning message concerns the behavior or situation that has generated the feeling. Usually the person who sends the communication implies, rather than explicitly states, the behavior or situation that creates the feeling. The intervener must try to infer what the behavior or situation is.

Rosenbluh (1981) explains that when another person communicates with you, distortion can occur in three areas:

1. What the other person means to say
2. What the other person actually says
3. What you, as the intervener, believe you hear

The present discussion is concerned with what interveners think they hear. The key to effective listening is accurately hearing the feeling and meaning behind the content of communication. The skill discussed here is *empathy.* Empathy is one's ability to enter the other person's world and to reflect this understanding to the person. Empathy, as Rosenbluh (1981) points out, contains two elements:

- *Passive:* The ability to hear the facts contained in the words and the feelings contained in the other person's body language, intensity, and tone
- *Active:* The ability to reflect this understanding to the other person in a manner that generates warmth, trust, and a willingness to be open

CLARIFICATION

Sometimes a victim will make a statement that the intervener does not fully understand. At other times, the victim's words and nonverbal behavior may not agree. At that point the intervener focuses on the misunderstanding and tries to clarify the statement in question before continuing with the interview. Interveners must never assume that they understand what the victim means. Two people can witness the same event and describe it very differently. Conversely, two people can have very different experiences and relate these experiences similarly. Interveners must be sure they know precisely what the victim is talking about. To do so, the intervener must press the sufferer to clarify any vague or ambiguous statements. An intervener cannot work effectively with a victim unless both the intervener and the victim are talking about the same crisis.

Clarification Techniques

Interveners can use the following four techniques to help victims clarify their statements:

1. *Repeating key words.* Using this technique, the intervener repeats key words or phrases that the victim uses and that the intervener does not clearly understand. By emphasizing a certain word or phrase, the intervener focuses attention on a particular thought or feeling and encourages the victim to explain it in more detail.

For example:

VICTIM: *I feel helpless when I think of all these bills . . . and I have no income.*
INTERVENER: *Helpless?*
VICTIM: *I just don't care anymore. I feel so isolated and depressed.*
INTERVENER: *You don't care anymore?* (or *You feel isolated?* or *You feel depressed?*)

Interveners should use this technique carefully. When used too frequently, repeating what the person just said can sound like a gimmick. The intervener's parroting could make the victim distrustful and uneasy. Repetition is, however, a useful tool when used cautiously.

2. *Restatement.* The intervener can rephrase the victim's statements in such a way that the person is encouraged to clarify what was said.

For example:

VICTIM: *I'm behind in all my bills, and my father, who is a local banker, told me it was embarrassing him because my creditors have been calling him, too.*
INTERVENER: *So you're having financial problems, and you are feeling heavy family pressure to find a solution.*

When an intervener uses restatement, the victim will often respond by talking about the most pressing area of concern. Using restatement also encourages the victim to explain the situation in more detail. This additional information will help the intervener understand what the victim is thinking and feeling.

3. *Direct method.* Perhaps the most direct method of eliciting information is for interveners to admit that they are confused or puzzled about the victim's statement and to ask the victim for clarification so that better understanding will result. This technique has the added advantage of letting the victim know that the intervener is interested in what is being said. In addition, this kind of communication helps build trust in the intervener-victim relationship.

4. *Asking questions.* An intervener can obtain a clearer idea of the other person's meaning simply by asking questions. When interveners want more information, they can ask "open" questions. To pinpoint specific items, interveners can ask "closed" questions. A *closed question* can be answered with a simple "yes" or "no." An *open question* allows for amplification of meaning by the respondent.

For example:

VICTIM: *I don't know what my husband is talking about.*
INTERVENER: *What does he say that you don't understand?* [open question]
VICTIM: *All I want is the best for my child. I am so miserable and feel so defeated that I want to kill myself.*
INTERVENER: *How would killing yourself help your child?* [open question]
or
Do you have a suicide plan in mind? [closed question]

The closed-question technique is particularly useful when an intervener is fairly sure of what additional information is needed.

Identifying the victim's concerns during the assessment and attempting to clarify the real issues involved help both the victim and the intervener better understand the total situation that must be dealt with.

USING QUESTIONS EFFECTIVELY

Asking questions to obtain accurate information in an intervention is both necessary and helpful. The intervener must be careful, however, to pace the questions carefully to avoid increasing the victim's stress level. Bombarding victims with a series of questions could confuse and frustrate them. Also, allow sufficient time for the victim to answer. Ask the questions in a nonthreatening, nonaccusatory tone.

DEALING WITH SILENCE

The intervener should know how to use silence during an intervention. For some interveners, silence is deadly. It may seem as if nothing is happening, and this can cause the intervener great discomfort. Interveners should handle silence by being silent themselves while observing the victim's behavior and what the victim is *not* saying.

RESPONDING EFFECTIVELY

Responding to another person's feelings is a delicate process. In gathering information from victims, the intervener must handle the victims' feelings with care and concern. If the intervener wants a victim to continue talking about facts pertinent to the problem, the intervener cannot judge, use logic, or give advice. The individual's feelings must be legitimized. The following example illustrates ineffective response to emotions:

> BOY: *I can't stand my father. He's been mean to me all my life.*
> INTERVENER: *That's unfair. What would you do if anything happened to him? You'd feel awful to have said things like that.*

In this instance, communication has been effectively shut off. The intervener has passed judgment and shamed the boy instead of seeking the root of the hostility. Here is another way to handle this situation:

> BOY: *I can't stand my father. He's been mean to me all my life.*
> INTERVENER: *Has your father done something mean recently?*
> BOY: *Yes.*

INTERVENER: *Would you tell me about that?*
BOY: *He wouldn't let me go to the game with my friends. I had to work.*
INTERVENER: *That upset you.*
BOY: *I just want to smash something. It's unfair. Everybody else got to go.*
INTERVENER: *What kind of work did you do?*
BOY: *All kinds of stuff that I was supposed to do last week.*
INTERVENER: *I'd like to hear about it.*

GUIDELINES FOR EFFECTIVE COMMUNICATIONS IN CRISES

1. Listen effectively.
    * Fully hear what the other person is saying.
    * Maintain eye contact if at all possible.
    * Let the other person talk freely.
    * Try to comprehend what the other person is saying.
    * Listen for both feelings and content.
    * Paraphrase the other's statements to gain clarification.
    * Ask for clarification when necessary.
    * Don't let your own feelings get in the way of understanding what the other person is trying to say.
2. Respond descriptively.
    * Don't be evaluative in your response; evaluative statements tend to elicit defensiveness.
    * Keep in mind that "rightness" or "wrongness" might not be the issue.
    * Remember, effective communication is not a contest; a "win or lose" mentality is inappropriate.
    * Learn all you can about the other person's thoughts and feelings.
    * Use descriptive statements and reveal your reactions to the other person.
3. Use your own feelings.
    * Remember that feelings are important in communicating and that they are always present.
    * Practice expressing your feelings.

- Take responsibility for your feelings.
- Use "I" messages rather than "you" messages; "I" messages reduce threat to the other person.
- Use descriptive statements that contain feelings.
- Be clear and specific about your feelings.

4. Assess needs.
   - Consider the needs of all involved.
   - Address issues over which the victim has actual control.
   - Avoid being judgmental and critical; avoid preaching.

5. Make timely responses.
   - Deliver responses at the time they are most important.
   - Deliver responses as soon as possible after the behavior that requires response.
   - Do not store up old concerns for later discussion.
   - Do not use old or saved concerns as a weapon.
   - Assess whether the other person is ready to handle your responses at this time.
   - Consider delaying responses on sensitive issues until you are in a more appropriate setting.
   - Discuss emotional issues in private.
   - Practice communication skills for greatest effectiveness.

LISTENING

During conversations with victims, keep in mind the following items about the importance of listening:

1. Listening is basic to successful communications.
2. Listening requires responsiveness.
3. Listening enables the listener to know more about the speaker.
4. Listening encourages expression.
5. Listening allows exploration of both feelings and content.
6. Listening helps establish trust between the parties.
7. Listening allows greater accuracy of communication.
8. Listening requires practice and is not always easy to learn.
9. Listening includes listening for content, feelings, and point of view.
10. Listening lets the speaker relax.

11. Listening enables the listener to watch for attitudes and feelings that might be conveyed nonverbally.

When you listen, remember to do the following:

1. Attend to verbal content.
2. Attend to nonverbal cues.
3. Hear and observe.
4. Attend to the feelings expressed by the speaker.
5. Don't think about other things when you are listening to someone.
6. Don't listen with only "half an ear."
7. Become attuned to the speaker's verbal and nonverbal messages.
8. Note any extra emphasis the speaker places on certain words.
9. Notice the speaker's speech patterns and recurring themes.

NONVERBAL COMMUNICATIONS

The following are examples of nonverbal acts a speaker may use to communicate:

- Sighing
- Flipping through papers
- Wincing
- Looking around, up, or down
- Smoking
- Chewing gum
- Yawning
- Tapping a finger or foot
- Frowning
- Displaying nervousness
- Avoiding eye contact
- Saying nothing
- Making jerky gestures
- Dressing sloppily
- Blinking rapidly
- Constantly looking at a clock or watch
- Showing favoritism

- Acting bored
- Being drunk

Certain nonverbal cues can indicate a specific attitude. Some examples follow.

Nonverbal Cues That Can Indicate Openness

- Uncrossed legs
- Open hands
- Unbuttoned coat, or unbuttoning the coat
- Hands spread apart
- Palms up
- Leaning forward

Nonverbal Cues That Can Indicate Defensiveness

- Fists closed
- Arms crossed in front of individual
- Legs crossed
- One leg over the chair arm

Nonverbal Cues That Can Indicate Cooperation

- Opening coat
- Head tilted
- Sitting on the edge of a chair
- Eye contact
- Hand-to-face gestures
- Leaning forward

Nonverbal Cues That Can Indicate Evaluating

- Head tilted
- Chin stroking
- Looking over glasses
- Pacing
- Pinching the bridge of the nose

Nonverbal Cues That Can Indicate Readiness

- Hands on hips
- Leaning forward

- Confident speech
- Moving closer to the other person

Nonverbal Cues That Can Indicate Suspicion

- Lack of eye contact
- Glancing sideways at the other person
- Body apparently pointed toward exit from area
- Touching the bridge of the nose
- Rubbing the ears
- Rubbing the eyes

Nonverbal Cues That Can Indicate Confidence

- Elevating oneself by sitting on a higher chair or standing on a platform
- Finger "steepling"
- Hands clasped behind the back
- Feet on a desk or table
- Leaning on an object
- Clucking sound
- Leaning back, with both hands supporting the neck

Both the following list and Figure 3.1 are guides that an intervener can show to victims who are having trouble identifying their feelings.

FEELINGS THAT PERSONS HAVE BUT OFTEN FAIL TO IDENTIFY

Abandoned	Blissful	Competitive
Adequate	Bold	Condemned
Affectionate	Bored	Confused
Ambivalent	Brave	Conspicuous
Angry	Calm	Contented
Annoyed	Capable	Cruel
Anxious	Challenged	Crushed
Apathetic	Charmed	Deceitful
Astounded	Cheated	Defeated
Awed	Cheerful	Delighted
Bad	Childish	Desirous
Betrayed	Clever	Despair
Bitter	Combative	Destructive

Determined	High	Pain
Different	Homesick	Panicked
Disappointed	Horrible	Peaceful
Discontented	Hurt	Persecuted
Distraught	Hysterical	Petrified
Disturbed	Ignored	Pity
Divided	Imposed upon	Pleasant
Dominated	Impressed	Pleased
Eager	Infatuated	Pressured
Ecstatic	Infuriated	Proud
Embarrassed	Inspired	Quarrelsome
Empty	Intimidated	Rage
Enchanted	Irritated	Refreshed
Energetic	Isolated	Rejected
Enjoyment	Jealousy	Relaxed
Envious	Joyous	Relieved
Evil	Jumpy	Remorse
Exasperated	Kind	Restless
Excited	Lazy	Righteous
Exhausted	Lecherous	Sad
Fascinated	Left out	Sated
Fearful	Lonely	Satisfied
Flustered	Longing	Scared
Foolish	Love	Screwed up
Frantic	Loving	Sexy
Free	Low	Shocked
Frightened	Lustful	Silly
Frustrated	Mad	Skeptical
Furious	Mean	Sneaky
Glad	Miserable	Solemn
Good	Mystical	Sorrowful
Gratified	Naughty	Spiteful
Greedy	Nervous	Startled
Grief	Nice	Stingy
Guilty	Nutty	Stuffed
Happy	Obnoxious	Stupid
Hate	Obsessed	Stunned
Heavenly	Odd	Suffering
Helpful	Outraged	Sure
Helpless	Overwhelmed	Sympathetic

Talkative
Tempted
Tense
Terrible
Terrified
Threatened
Tired

Trapped
Troubled
Ugly
Uneasy
Unsettled
Violent
Vehement

Vulnerable
Vivacious
Weepy
Wicked
Wonderful
Worried

AGGRESSIVE   ANXIOUS   APOLOGETIC   ARROGANT   BLISSFUL

BORED   CONFIDENT   ECSTATIC   ENRAGED   EXASPERATED

EXHAUSTED   FRUSTRATED   GUILTY   HUNGOVER   HYSTERICAL

INDIFFERENT   INNOCENT   INTERESTED   LOADED   LONELY

LOVESTRUCK   MEDITATIVE   MISERABLE   NEGATIVE   OPTIMISTIC

SATISFIED   SURLY   TURNED-ON   TURNED-OFF   WITHDRAWN

FIGURE **3.1**

How do you feel today?

TEAM INTERVENTION

TEAM INTERVENTION RESPONSIBILITIES AND PROCEDURES

Although many crisis situations can be effectively handled by a single intervener, some circumstances dictate the use of a team of interveners or multiple teams of interveners. The importance of the team concept rests in its potential for providing maximum safety for all involved, for efficient information gathering from the crisis victims, for division of responsibility among the team members, and for emotional and physical support for the team members. Effective team intervention requires that each team member accept personal responsibility for his or her share of the team effort. Failure to acknowledge and assume this responsibility could exacerbate the crisis and jeopardize the safety of the other team members. Because of the number of people being managed (both victims and interveners), team interventions must be carefully and thoughtfully orchestrated. This chapter deals with the designation and role of lead teams and lead interveners, the division of responsibility of the interveners, and the positioning of the team members as part of the Crisis Intervention procedure.

Crisis Intervention can be done by a single intervener, a team of interveners, or multiple teams of interveners (see Figure 4.1). The decision to use a single intervener, a team, or multiple teams will be dictated by the number of crisis victims involved in the particular situation and the nature of the situation. The greater the number of victims and the more potentially hostile the circumstance is, the greater the need is for the control and safety backup that multiple teams can offer. A family dispute involving two members might require a team intervention.

A large family dispute involving significant others might necessitate multiple teams. A dispute between two students might be handled effectively by a single intervener or by a team. A playground dispute involving the primary victims, bystanders, hecklers, and other agitators will require multiple teams.

Effective intervention in a crisis situation requires that an intervener be emotionally and physically prepared to intervene in the situation at hand. The intervener must ask several important questions in determining his or her readiness. These questions include the following:

1. Is this an intervention that I can emotionally and physically handle?
2. Will personal, unresolved biases or prejudices interfere with my ability to be effective? (The most blatant example of bias

Single intervener intervention

Single team intervention

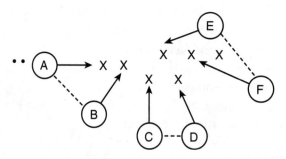

Multiple team intervention

FIGURE 4.1

A,B,C,D,E,F = Crisis Interveners
X's = Victims
------- = Team Relationships
•• = Control or Lead Intervener

often exists in child abuse cases, where the intervener might not be willing to acknowledge the crisis being experienced by the abuser and might focus only on the crisis of the child. This attitude can potentiate crisis for the intervener and increase the stress level of those already in crisis.)

3. Will my physical safety be in jeopardy if I intervene in this situation? Do we need additional support personnel before we enter the situation?
4. Is the line of communication between my partner and me fail-safe?
5. Can I depend on my partner?

The intervener who experiences ambiguity in the answers and is unwilling to resolve the problems immediately risks sabotaging his or her effectiveness and putting him- or herself and the partner in danger. Lack of clarity could exacerbate the suffering of the victims and also cause the intervener to go into crisis.

If, however, the intervener and partner are clear about their goal, reasonably certain of their safety, in agreement on team procedure, and prepared to intervene regardless of the situation, then they should proceed with the intervention.

While team and multiple team interventions follow the six basic steps of Crisis Intervention procedure—(1) immediacy, (2) control, (3) assessment, (4) disposition, (5) referral, and (6) follow-up—team members have specific responsibilities inherent in the team structure.

The following is an outline of the procedure and the team members' responsibilities within the procedure.

Immediacy

Intervention Procedure In approaching a crisis, the immediacy of the intervention is vital. The team must attempt to relieve anxiety, prevent further disorientation, and ensure that the victims do not harm themselves or others.

Control

Intervention Procedure The necessity for adequate situational controls differs little from that needed in any type of crisis intervention attempt. The additional factors in a team approach are related to the number of victims involved, the increased possibility of hostility, the group dynamics, and the increase in the amount of information that must be received and understood by the interveners. Proper control procedures protect the victims of crisis, the interveners, significant others, and bystanders and assist in defusing the high-pitched emotional tone present in almost all crises.

Responsibilities of Team Members

1. Team A is the lead team. Intervener A is the lead intervener.
2. Decide before entering the crisis situation which team member will intervene with which victim. Time is limited. The decision must be made quickly and on the basis of on-the-spot assessment and past experience. Often the interveners' skills and experience in the particular situation determine the pairing. Regardless of how the designation is made, the interveners must follow the game plan. A faltering entrance, with interveners unsure of their positions, will cause additional confusion and chaos.
3. The teams must give an impression of structure.
4. In multiple interventions Team A will enter first and begin the intervention process with the designated victims. Team B will observe and assess the situation, then move in at the direction of its team leader. The goal of Team B is to complement and support Team A's effort, not compete with the process already begun. Team C will move in as appropriate.
5. If it seems prudent for the interveners to switch victims, eye signals and hand signals may be used to direct the switch. This strategy can be done effectively if eye contact between the interveners is maintained.
6. The Team A leader must carefully assess the situation before deciding to make a switch. If Team B members have gained control and begun establishing rapport with their victims, it is counterproductive to interrupt the process. The bottom line is always a commitment to the needs and concerns of the victims, not to technique gimmickry.
7. Avoid leaving victims unattended. Being left alone increases the possibility of the victims renewing the conflict, harming themselves or others, or feeling helpless and isolated again. Interveners must maintain the trust of the victims.

8. All teams must be prepared for the unexpected. When emotions are charged, behavior is often unpredictable. When numerous people are involved, one person's irrational act can trigger a domino effect. A sudden flare-up or new crisis can occur at any point during the intervention. The teams must be aware of this possibility and be ready to respond. This might require reintervening or starting over again to gain control, and then moving to the assessment process. The team's calm self-control and patience will mean the difference between reducing the stress and tension and exacerbating the new crisis. This underscores the need for team members and member teams to remain in contact and to know where each team is positioned. Such emotional and physical support translates into intervener survival as well as into effective intervention.

9. In a dispute involving large numbers, team leaders should identify the victim who requires the most urgent attention and begin intervening with him or her. Teams B and C will then move in to intervene where necessary.

10. When control has been established, the Team A leader will convene other team leaders to exchange information and to move to the assessment phase.

Assessment

Intervention Procedure

1. The lead intervener A gathers information from the crisis victim, while team member B monitors verbal and nonverbal information. Body language is an important source of information and should be noted.

2. When necessary, team member B asks for further information to clarify what has been said.

3. As appropriate, team member B intervenes separately with a victim. For example, in a family dispute it is often prudent to intervene with a young child or children separately from the other family members so the intervener can establish rapport with the child or children. Interveners often make the mistake of excluding children from the intervention process even when the problem centers on them, or when they are in crisis themselves. It is often assumed that children

who are not crying, who are not visibly upset, or who do not request help must be handling the situation like "big people." By attending to children during the crisis period, the intervener will help effectively manage problems that might otherwise continue to surface throughout their adulthoods. For a variety of reasons, including intimidation, ambivalent loyalties, and confusion, children might not be willing to express them-selves in the family group. In a one-on-one situation, a sensitive, caring intervener can help children articulate pressing problems.

4. A family crisis situation may involve significant others such as grandparents, in-laws, or other relatives who are present when the interveners arrive at the scene. As appropriate, intervener B can intervene with significant others, either within the room or in a separate area of the room.

5. If the group is large, the primary team may find it necessary to bring in another team. Disputes on a school yard, a crisis in a shopping center, disputes during an athletic event will all attract and involve large numbers of people. A single intervener might need additional backup to maintain control and to intervene effectively.

6. During the assessment, the team members will confer to share information and to determine an appropriate time to bring the disputants or victims together again.

Responsibilities of Team Members

1. Maintain eye contact with each other to ensure mutual protection.

2. Have clearly defined signals concerning caucusing and switching victims.

3. Have a clearly defined understanding of individual roles before entering the situation. Competition, hidden agendas, and power plays among interveners will sabotage an intervention. There must be clarity of rules and a unity of purpose if the intervention is to be effective. Generally, the lead intervener is designated by mutual consent of the team; the lead team is the first team on the scene. Any changes made during the intervention process must be arranged

carefully and smoothly to avoid confusion and or escalating
the crisis.

4. Avoid interrupting the other interveners or the victims.
5. Avoid crossing a verbal transaction between intervener and
   victim or introducing a competing idea during a transaction.
   Crisis victims require structure and clarity. To create additional confusion by asking many questions in rapid succession or by asking conflicting questions is counterproductive.
   The interveners must listen to each other. Caucus or signal
   the other team members if their approaches are obviously
   not helpful.
6. Caucus as appropriate to share information and to develop
   strategy. The caucus must be brief; a lengthy meeting
   could renew feelings of isolation, fear, and mistrust in the
   victim.
7. Identify the nature of the precipitating events. If intervener A
   is responsible for interviewing both or all victims, intervener B should attend to the information and give feedback to intervener A. Intervener B should ask for clarification if necessary and generally support the efforts of
   intervener A.
8. Team members must be reassuring and calm, maintaining a
   certain steadiness and warmth toward the crisis victims.
   They must be attentive and empathetic and be willing to
   reach out to the victims both emotionally and physically if
   needed.

Disposition

Intervention Procedure

1. In agreement with the other team members, the lead intervener A will bring the victims together to discuss the particular problems that they are experiencing.
2. Lead intervener A will request each victim to articulate the
   problem as he or she perceives it. Intervener A must insist that
   that the speaker not be interrupted by the other party or
   parties.

3. Help the victims develop or reinstitute adaptive coping mechanisms. Help the victims move from maladaptive behavior to more realistic and effective functioning. Help the victims mobilize their own resources and explore options. Crisis victims experience difficulty in perceiving options in their lives. This feeling of being helpless and impotent heightens stress and ultimately creates the crisis. The intervener must help the victims recognize available, viable options for managing their problems.

4. Intervention teams must try to build a sense of structure that the victims can relate to. The more that the victims understand, and the more that they can begin to secure a sense of control and structure, the sooner they will be able to regain their self-control and function effectively.

Responsibilities of Team Members

1. Seat victims and interveners carefully to create an atmosphere conducive to problem management.
2. Intervener B should support lead intervener A's efforts to maintain control. Minimize interruptions.
3. Do not cross transactions.
4. Clarify and simplify; do not create additional or new confusion.
5. In offering options, allow the victims sufficient time to digest an idea. Avoid battering victims with many ideas in rapid succession. Move slowly and thoughtfully to eliminate confusion or frustration.
6. Learn to be comfortable with silence. Do not prolong the procedure out of a fear that silence might be seen as impotence or lack of interest by the intervener. If lead intervener A is successfully directing the procedure, intervener B should support that effort. Concern, interest, and empathy can be communicated by nonverbal behavior as well as by verbal expression.

Referral

Intervention Procedure The interveners have as their main concerns the immediate crisis problems rather than those that might be chronic and not immediately present. Often, however, the interveners must make a proper referral subsequent to the intervention. With only a short time to intervene effectively and to discuss referrals, it is important that the team be prepared to make efficient and effective suggestions for additional help where needed.

Responsibilities of Team Members

1. Each member of the team should have an updated referral list of resources that provides correct current addresses, phone numbers, availability of staff, hours of operation, cost of services, qualifications for obtaining services, available transportation to the referral agency, and the name of a contact person at the agency.
2. In consultation, the team members should determine which referral or referrals would be most appropriate under the circumstances.
3. Team leader A should assume responsibility for obtaining a verbal commitment from the victim that he or she will call at a particular time to set up an appointment with the agency. If possible, have the victim make the call while the intervener is present to give support.
4. Team member B should assume responsibility for giving the victim a card or paper with the name, address, phone number, and contact person at the referral agency.

Follow-up

One of the team members should assume responsibility for follow-up to determine if the appointment was made, if the victim kept the appointment, and if there were any problems.

It is strongly suggested that

1. Teams of interveners should be created within agencies, organizations, schools, hospitals. Smooth team functioning results from the experience of working together and training together.
2. Wherever possible, the intervention teams should establish a method of debriefing within their organization or agency. Having someone available to listen to feelings and concerns is a key to intervener survival. The debriefing can also be used as an opportunity to share new approaches, reinforce ideas, and to strengthen skills.

A POTPOURRI OF MISTAKEN ASSUMPTIONS

"If You Can't Help Them, at Least Don't Hurt Them."

The assumption here is that there can be a "noneffect" of intervention on the sufferer. This is not so. When one intervenes in another person's crisis, that person will either be helped or hurt as a result of the intervention. Under no circumstances will the sufferer be unaffected. The effect, whether positive or negative, will be determined by what the intervener does or does not do. Therefore, knowing when to stay out is as important as knowing when to become involved. There is no shame in not intervening if you decide that your skills are inadequate in a particular situation or that your own psychological well-being is at stake. If you decide to intervene in a situation that you cannot handle, however, your involvement will worsen the situation. Your decision to intervene requires you to accept that your action will have some direct, important impact on the person in crisis.

"I Know Exactly How You Feel."

Even under the best conditions, this is doubtful. If you say you know and you really do not, your credibility as an intervener is destroyed. If you make such a statement to a victim, be prepared to back it up with accurate information about the sufferer's feelings. Making assumptions about the sufferer's feelings too early in the intervention can prove disastrous. Victims of a crisis often want to talk to someone, but they will not talk indiscriminately. Being in crisis does not preclude testing the sincerity of those who say they want to help. The victim can challenge your assumption by saying, "OK, how do I feel?" or "How can you know how I feel? We just met!" The unprepared intervener might have to do some fast backpedaling.

"If I Ask About Suicide, the Person Might Do It."

Wrong again! The victim from whom you receive signals about suicide is already considering it. In fact, even if the person is not considering suicide, the fact that you are open about the subject may make it easier to talk about in the future. Almost all of us have at least had passing thoughts about what suicide is or how it could affect us. For the sufferer contemplating a suicidal act, your use of the term *suicide* may make it less frightening and therefore easier to talk about. If you are not afraid to use the term, maybe the sufferer does not have to be uncomfortable with it either. Be assured that using the terms *suicide* or *killing yourself* will not cause the act to happen.

"I Can Relax After the Parties Are Seated."

Never relax during an intervention! Although it is true that it is harder to remain physically aggressive while seated, never underestimate your situation or its potential for violence. An eruption can occur at any time and can affect you directly and severely. Having to be "on your toes" all the time is a major reason that Crisis Intervention can be physically and emotionally exhausting to the intervener as well as to the victim. Not everyone can perform Crisis Intervention effectively. If you are going to intervene effectively, be prepared for the drain on your energy and stamina.

"Listening to and Acknowledging Feelings Implies That I Agree with the Victim and the Victim's Behavior."

Relationships are not built on agreement; they are built on understanding. Serious disagreements can exist within a close personal relationship if both parties know that each will take the time to understand the other. Similarly, with a person in crisis, it is possible to listen and respond to feelings even though you do not agree with the person's actions. In fact, sometimes you may need to tell the person about your nonagreement. This honesty will not interfere with the relationship-building necessary to the intervention or subsequent referral. Rather, the intervention could gain even greater strength because of your ability to differentiate between feelings and agreement. Also, remember that victims' asking for agreement with their actions can be a way of testing the intervener's sincerity and honesty. The intervener's credibility is at issue here.

"My Degree, Badge, or Profession Will Automatically Make Me an Effective Intervener."

Unfortunately, this has long been thought to be the case. It was often assumed that if you were a good therapist, for example, that you were also a qualified crisis intervener. Practice has demonstrated repeatedly that one must learn and apply Crisis Intervention skills as a separate discipline rather than as the stepchild of some other part of the behavioral sciences. Although psychologists, counselors, mediators, psychiatrists, or social workers may make excellent crisis interveners in many settings, the fact that one has such a title does not in itself ensure skilled crisis management. Often, those most skilled in Crisis Intervention have not been trained in any of the behavioral science disciplines. Professional training may make us skilled professionals in our fields, but it might not qualify us to apply what we know in ways specific to Crisis Intervention.

SPECIAL ISSUES

SAFETY FOR THE INTERVENER

During an intervention, the crisis intervener's safety is a major consideration. The possibility of injury to the intervener exists regardless of professional capacity. For that reason, we suggest the following safety procedures. The procedures must be adapted to each individual crisis situation and to the intervener's skill and training.

Out of the Office

1. If possible, always intervene with a partner. This is especially important when there is more than one victim or disputant.
2. Approach the crisis or potential crisis slowly and carefully. If you are approaching a house, building, or room, take time to survey the surroundings for clues that might help later. Although time is critical in Crisis Intervention, the precautions you take at the outset could prevent problems later.
3. If you are in a car, do not park directly in front of the area where the crisis is occurring. Assess what is happening around you as you leave your vehicle. Be observant at all times.
4. Approach all doors or openings with caution. Do not stand directly in front of doors or windows. Stand to one side, and, only then, knock on the door. Interveners have been killed or injured during family disputes by bullets fired through a door in response to the intervener's knock.

5. Before knocking or ringing the doorbell, listen for 10 to 15 seconds for additional clues that could help you as you enter the situation. These could include screaming, objects being broken, weapons being fired, angry voices, or threats. Perhaps you will hear no noise at all.

6. Once the door is opened, maintain control of the situation by keeping everyone involved in front of you and within eyesight.

7. Perform a visual "frisk" of all persons in the room to determine if weapons are hidden in pockets, belts, shoes, and so on. Pay attention!!

8. Observe the persons in crisis. What are they doing? What must you do immediately to stabilize the situation? Do it!

9. Note any objects in the room that could be used in a violent way. A heavy ashtray or an innocent letter opener could become a lethal weapon in the hands of a violent person.

10. Be aware of all other persons in the room, and note all persons who enter after you arrive. Assume nothing. Observe both the verbal and nonverbal behavior of everyone in the room. Find out who else is in the house and their locations, if possible.

11. Be prepared for unexpected behavior of significant others, neighbors, or visitors in the house.

12. Initially, step into the room only a few feet at a time. Proceed only as far as it seems safe.

13. If necessary, separate the disputants. Avoid using the kitchen, bedroom, or bathroom; weapons are often stored in those areas.

14. Gain control as quickly as possible. You may use anything short of physical force, as appropriate and according to your training. A shrill whistle, a loud clap, a loud voice, an absurd request under the circumstances (asking permission to use a phone book, for example), or other attention-getting device may be used for this purpose.

15. Have the victims sit down. The failure of disputants to sit does not preclude a successful intervention; however, the potential for violence and aggression seems to be lower when everyone is seated.

16. Select an appropriate place to sit so you can maintain your own safety, gain and maintain control of the situation, and proceed with the intervention.

17. Visually assess the room and the adjoining areas, if possible.
18. Know where entrances and exits are.
19. Know where you might get assistance should you need it. Is there a working telephone in the room? Do you have a portable phone or radio?
20. Sit in the following manner: feet solidly on the floor with heels and toes touching the floor; hands unfolded in your lap; your body leaning slightly forward toward the victim. This position accomplishes two important functions:
    a. It gives the victim the feeling that you are attentive to what is being said and experienced. Your body language conveys a sense of interest and concern.
    b. It permits you to respond immediately should you be physically threatened. Although a crossed-leg, folded-arm position, or a similarly relaxed position might be more comfortable, it can reduce your ability to respond quickly should an immediate response be needed.
21. Attempt to speak with the crisis victim at eye level.
22. Avoid standing above the victim in an authoritarian or parental manner. If the victim chooses to remain standing, you should remain standing also.
23. Do not turn your back on a crisis victim or allow the victim to walk behind you.
24. Do not position yourself in a corner from which you cannot exit if necessary.
25. Remove any objects or extraneous clothing parts that a violent victim could use against you. Name tags connected by pins; pens and pencils; regular, non clip-on neckties; scarves; and jewelry, such as chain necklaces or hoop earrings, are all potential weapons in the wrong hands.
26. Stand in the following manner: feet placed shoulder width apart; one foot slightly behind the other; weight on the rear leg; knees slightly bent; hands folded, but not interlocked, on the upper abdomen or lower chest; arms unfolded. This unrestricted stance permits instant response to a physical threat. Hands placed in one's pockets are suspect, and having to remove your hands from your pockets increases your response time. Folded arms can be threatening and can also impede your response. Maintaining your weight on the rear leg with

knees slightly bent permits quick movement in almost any direction without affecting balance.

27. Once separated, bring the disputants back together as soon as it seems productive to do so.

28. Maintain eye contact with your partner and attempt to break eye contact between the disputants as soon as possible.

In the Office

1. In the office, allow for maximum personal safety by doing the following:

    a. Remove potential weapons such as heavy ashtrays, paperweights, letter openers, scissors, and the like.

    b. Arrange seating so that victims have access to the exit without going over you.

    c. When you greet victims, notice anything strange or unusual about their words, actions, or dress. Allow your senses to give you clues, and take all clues seriously until you have been able to rule them out.

    d. Observe the victims' body language as they enter.

    e. Enter the room behind the victims. Visually "frisk" the victims.

    f. If possible, arrange several seating areas within the room that can be used as needed with different threat levels.

    g. Do not remain after hours with a potentially violent victim unless proper security is available.

    h. Arrange a "buddy system" so that someone is available should you need help.

    i. If you know that the victims are involved in situations where there is a potential for violence, arrange to have a co-intervener in the office with you, or at least close at hand. As appropriate, inform the victim about other persons available.

    j. After hours, enter your office in the same careful manner that you would enter a crisis victim's house.

    k. Enter elevators only after checking for other passengers.

    l. Know your emergency telephone numbers and use them if you need help. Do not hesitate.

2. If at all possible, always intervene with a partner.

3. Make contingency plans for all interventions. Consider what you would do under a variety of conditions. Learn to play the "what if" game. Play it often. Preplanning will affect automatic behavior under stress.
4. Always take safety precautions seriously. The intervention and your life may depend on your behavior in this regard.
5. Be familiar with the cultures present in the community so that you can respond appropriately and sensitively.

GUIDELINES FOR INCREASING THE CRISIS INTERVENER'S MULTICULTURAL AWARENESS[1]

1. Attempt to become aware of your own cultural biases.
2. If possible, learn the language of those into whose crisis you might need to intervene. Find a qualified translator if necessary.
3. Ask for clarification if you are not sure what the victim said.
4. Do not assume that you understand any nonverbal communication unless you are familiar with the victim's culture.
5. Do not impose your personal values.
6. If the victim's nonverbal communication is insulting in your culture, do not take it personally.
7. Develop an awareness of anything in your own nonverbal communication that might be insulting in certain cultures.
8. Make every effort to increase your awareness of your own preconceptions and stereotypes of the cultures you may encounter.
9. With your increased awareness, reinterpret the behavior of people from another culture from *their* cultural perspective.
10. Be willing to test, adapt, and change your perceptions to fit your new experience.
11. Maintain objectivity.
12. Recognize that you cannot change a person's cultural perspectives.

---

[1] Partially adapted from *A Handbook for Developing Multicultural Awareness* (pp. 23–25) by P. A. Pederson, 1988, New York: American Association for Counseling and Development.

13. Do not judge people from another culture by your own cultural values until you have come to know the people and their cultural values.
14. Recognize that your lack of familiarity with a victim's culture might increase the stress within the intervention.
15. Clarify your role, knowledge, and experience with the parties so you maintain the integrity demanded by your position as intervener.

IDENTIFYING STUDENTS AT RISK FOR VIOLENT BEHAVIOR[2]

The following checklists of "early warning signs" will aid in identifying students who might need intervention. The more items that are checked, the greater the potential is for violent acting-out behavior.

Children and adolescents at risk might

- Express self-destructive or homicidal ideation
- Have a history of self-destructive behavior
- Articulate specific plans to harm self or others
- Engage in "bullying" other children
- Have difficulty with impulse control
- Evidence significant changes in behavior
- Engage in substance abuse
- Become involved with gangs
- Evidence a preoccupation with fighting
- Have a history of antisocial behavior
- Evidence a low tolerance for frustration
- Externalize blame for their difficulties
- Have harmed small animals
- Have engaged in fire setting
- Evidence persistent bed wetting
- Appear to be or acknowledge feeling depressed
- Talk about not being around
- Express feelings of hopelessness
- Give away possessions
- Appear withdrawn

---

[2] Reprinted with permission from *A Practical Guide for Crisis Response in Our Schools* 1999 by the American Academy of Experts in Traumatic Stress, 368 Veterans Memorial Highway, Commack, New York 11725.

- Evidence significant changes in mood
- Experience sleep and eating disturbances
- Have experienced prior trauma or tragedy
- Have been or are victims of child abuse
- Have experienced a significant loss
- Evidence a preoccupation with television programs or movies with violent themes
- Evidence a preoccupation with games with violent themes
- Evidence a preoccupation with guns and other weapons
- Have access to a firearm
- Have brought a weapon to school
- Evidence frequent disciplinary problems
- Exhibit poor academic performance
- Have been frequently truant from school

The American Psychological Association (APA & MTV, 1999) has compiled a list of nine signs that a child is likely to become violent. Each individual factor is important to consider; however, clusters of factors might be more indicative.

APA WARNING SIGNS

- Loss of temper on a daily basis
- Frequent physical fighting
- Significant vandalism or property damage
- Increase in the use of drugs or alcohol
- Increase in risk-taking behavior
- Detailed plans to commit acts of violence
- Threatening to hurt others
- Enjoying hurting animals
- Carrying a weapon

The American Academy of Child and Adolescent Psychiatry (APA & MTV, 1999) has also developed a list of factors that might help identify at-risk children. Although no set of factors is absolute, all behavior has meaning. Understanding that meaning helps teachers and interveners help students.

AACAP WARNING SIGNS

- Previous aggressive or violent behavior
- Being the victim of physical abuse, sexual abuse, or both

- Exposure to violence in the home or in the community
- Having a parent who is violent
- Heavy exposure to violence on television or in movies
- Use of drugs and alcohol
- Presence of firearms in the home
- Brain damage from head injury

IDENTIFYING ADULTS AT RISK FOR VIOLENT BEHAVIOR

The following checklist can give important clues to the potential for violent acts by those in whom they are observed. Although there is no single or simplistic answer to the problem, greater awareness of some of the factors involved can help in planning and response to such potential behavior. As the number of factors increase, the likelihood of violent behavior may also increase, even though the type of violent behavior might not be apparent. Observation of only a few factors does not preclude violence. Conversely, multiple factors do not predict with certainty that violence is imminent.

- Historical problems, singular or serial, are severe enough to warrant police intervention.
- The person expresses feelings of powerlessness to effect the outcome of his or her dispute with another.
- The situation experienced by the person is the result of a family dispute or divorce, especially if children are involved.
- There is a history of causing deliberate encounters with the police or confrontations with other authorities relative to a personal case before the court or in relation to orders of the court.
- There is current or historical use of minor children as a tool, pawn, or weapon against the other spouse in a family dispute.
- The conflict experienced involves allegations of child abuse or spouse abuse.
- Where there are allegations of abuse, a complaint has been filed by either or both parties that has been or is about to be presented in court.
- Direct threats have been made from one party against the other or by third parties against either or both parties.

- There is a history of difficult court appearances or ineffective legal battles.
- Persons show an unusual interest in or expenditures of limited personal resources for reforming an inadequate, unfair or unjust judicial, social, professional or employment system. Such interests or expenditures seem disproportionate to other activities in the person's life.
- The person has a history of recent multiple life stressors either directly related or unrelated to the current conflict experienced.
- The person indicates high levels of personal dissatisfaction with his or her life.
- The cultural background of the actor emphasizes a major importance of "loss of face" or of male dominance in relationships.
- The person has a perceived or actual lack of personal support systems. He or she might be seen as a loner or as interested in non-human interactions
- The person makes verbalizations concerning homicide or suicide.
- The verbalizations concern the taking and holding of hostages, especially family members.
- The verbalizations concern "setting affairs in order" or sound like the making of a "verbal will."
- The person has a history of impulsive acts.
- Those observing the person have an intuitive feeling that something is about to happen of a violent nature.
- The person has recently purchased a weapon and ammunition absent a historical interest in such items.
- The person has a history of high interest in weapons coupled with substantial recent purchases of weapons or ammunition.
- The person has a history of perceived or actual multiple personal losses.
- The person has a history of multiple life changes within a relatively short time period.
- The person has a diagnosed psychiatric disorder.
- The person shows inappropriately subdued affect or behavior that is an inconsistent reaction to the actual issues at hand.
- The person has a history of perceived violent acts.
- The person has a history of violent acts with animals during childhood.

- The person's developmental history indicates a lack of early, constant, and nurturant attachments.
- The person grew up within an impulsive family structure or in an overly controlled family.
- Violence in subject's family of orientation is seen as a mode of communication.
- The peer group of the subject endorses violence.
- The person has a history of or current job instability.
- The person has a medical history of central nervous system trauma or current subjective CNS symptoms such as complaints of dizziness, blackouts, amnesia, memory loss, headaches, nausea, episodic rage, or sense of confusion with remorse.
- The person shows objective central nervous system signs.

INTERVENER SURVIVAL

High stress levels, personal frustration, and inadequate coping skills have major personal, organizational, and social costs. Stress is not a mental illness, but a part of everyday living. Each of us is potentially vulnerable to the problems of too much stress and too little coping ability.

SIGNS AND SYMPTOMS OF STRESS AND BURNOUT

1. High resistance to going to work every day
2. A pervasive sense of failure, as indicated by such expressions as "I can't do enough"; "I can't get it right"; "I'm no good anymore."
3. Anger and resentment.
4. Guilt and blame. These might be expressed by such expressions as, "No matter how many hours I work, I never finish, and I feel guilty about leaving. I'm in a 'no-win' situation."
5. Discouragement and indifference.
6. Negativism.
7. Isolation and withdrawal.
8. Feelings of tiredness and exhaustion that last all day.
9. Frequent clock watching.
10. Extreme fatigue after work.
11. Loss of positive feelings toward victims.
12. Postponement of victim contacts; resistance to client phone calls and office visits.
13. Inability to concentrate or listen to information.
14. Feelings of immobilization.

15. Cynicism toward victims, co-workers, or the world in general.
16. Sleep disorders, including difficulty either in falling asleep or in staying asleep, or sleeping an adequate amount but not feeling rested upon waking. These disorders occur regularly over an extended period.
17. Self-preoccupation.
18. Becoming more approving of behavior-control measures, such as tranquilizers.
19. Frequent colds and flus.
20. Frequent headaches and gastrointestinal disturbances.
21. Rigidity in thinking and resistance to change.
22. Suspicion and paranoia.
23. Excessive drug use.
24. Marital and family conflict.
25. Free-floating anxiety, evidenced by such expressions as, "I'm constantly worried and anxious, but I can't pinpoint what I'm upset about. It just seems to hover there."
26. Tunnel vision: as stress increases, perception of available options narrows.
27. A sense of increasing helplessness.
28. Fear that "it won't get better."
29. Fear of losing control.
30. High absenteeism.

Intervener and victim alike are subject to stressors, and both can become incapacitated as a result of unmanaged stress.

A person in crisis cannot assist another person who is also in crisis.

Ensuring Intervener Survival

Intervener survival addresses the needs and concerns of the intervener in preparation for, or in the actual performance of, intervention in a crisis. It is not sufficient to learn crisis management procedures without attending to the sources of stress and tension that could impinge on the intervener. Such tension can affect the intervener's ability to intervene effectively and efficiently. Interveners who experience a personal crisis while trying to help others who are also in crisis are of no help to anyone, least of all themselves.

In intervening in the crises of others, the interveners sometimes neglect personal needs, health and nutrition, personal safety, and responsibility for self-direction. Interveners might become so involved in others' lives that they forget to pay attention to themselves. Continually discounting personal needs, or failing to value oneself as one values those being helped, can interfere with effectiveness. In addition, the intervener could experience physical and emotional harm. If interveners neglect concern for personal safety during interventions or fail to recognize that they are experiencing stress, productivity and efficiency will suffer.

Conversely, if interveners are aware of these areas and have spent the time and energy needed to attend to them, they will be better prepared to focus on the crises of others. Regardless of the intervener's attempt to disavow ownership for feelings of frustration, anger, stress, and tension, these feelings and the resulting behavior remain a personal responsibility.

The following are suggestions for keeping stress within tolerable limits:

1. Eliminate stressor foods from your diet. Nutritional stress can be as debilitating as emotional stress.
2. Get enough rest and sleep.
3. Exercise regularly and appropriately for your age and fitness level.
4. Be realistic about the givens of your world. Work within the reality of "what is" today.
5. Realistically assess what you are able to do in your particular situation.
6. Schedule time for fun. Allow time each day to experience good feelings.
7. Schedule time each week for dreaming, thinking, wandering, exploring, planning, and being in touch with your dreams.
8. Schedule regular recreation or vacation time. The quantity of time spent is not important; the quality of time spent in recreation is the key to stress reduction.
9. Be sure you get your minimum daily requirement of positive nurturing.
10. Set realistic goals in all areas of your life.
11. Consider the following carefully:
    a. Everything I do is the result of a choice I make.

b. Every choice I make benefits me positively in some way, even though I may not know what the benefit is at the moment.

c. I have inside me everything I need and all the tools I need to guide my life successfully.

d. I can choose to gain greater self-awareness.

e. I am responsible for 100% of my life.

f. The degree to which others control my life is the degree to which I allow them to control it.

g. I cannot voluntarily change my feelings, but I can always voluntarily change my behavior.

h. Any problem I experience in my life is a problem I have created for myself.

i. If I choose to continue creating a particular problem for myself, I do it because
    (1) I receive some pleasure or unacknowledged benefit or payoff for continuing the problem, or
    (2) I can avoid a greater or more fearful problem by perpetuating the current problem. In other words, if I solve the current problem, I am afraid the greater problem will occur.

The need for caring, well-trained supervisors who can effectively help to reduce the heightened stress experienced by their peers and their staff is being recognized by cost-conscious organizations. Retaining trained personnel makes sense. Stress management programs in a workplace environment require the support and encouragement of supervisors and management. Employees will not participate unless they feel safe in doing so.

CRITICAL INCIDENT STRESS MANAGEMENT

The main focus of Critical Incident Stress Management (CISM) is the emergency service worker and not the primary victim of the crisis situation. Mitchell (1983) points out that critical incidents produce a characteristic set of responses both psychological and physiological. The symptoms manifested in such circumstances are normal and expected reactions to abnormal and unexpected situations. Although the reactions might be normal, if the stress is not effectively dealt with, the workers could experience both long- and short-term psychological and physical debilitation.

CISM is divided into several modalities according to Dr. Mitchell. These include the following:

1. *Initial defusing* performed within eight hours of the critical incident and provided at a place away from the scene of the incident. A defusing is targeted for the core personnel most affected by the event. Defusing is a shortened version of the Critical Incident Stress Debriefing (CISD) and consists of only three phases: Introduction, Exploration, and Information. The defusing provides an opportunity to check on the well-being of personnel involved, provide encouragement, and make decisions about whether or not a debriefing is going to be required. Trained critical incident stress team members provide the defusing.

2. *CISD* is a structured group meeting, about a distressing critical incident, usually taking place 24–72 hours after the incident. Based on principles of education and crisis intervention, CISD is a peer driven, clinician-guided discussion intended to mitigate the incident and accelerate recovery from significant stress related to a traumatic event. The CISD consists of seven phases: Introduction, Fact, Thought, Reaction, Symptom, Teaching, and Reentry (see Mitchell & Everly [1996] for step-by-step guidelines of CISD).

3. *Demobilization* is a brief intervention reserved for use immediately after a disaster or large-scale incident. Demobilization provides a transition period from the world of the traumatic event back to normal functions. As units are disengaged from operations at the scene of the disaster, they are sent to the demobilization center for a 10-minute talk on critical incident stress and possible symptoms they might encounter. Workers hear concrete stress-management suggestions, which will be immediately helpful to them until a CISD can be arranged. After the 10-minute talk, personnel move to another room where food and drink are available. After a 20-minute rest, the workers either return to normal duties or home.

4. *Follow-up CISD.* Follow-up CISD can be done several weeks post incident or post formal CISD. The educational nature of CISD might need to be extended if the problems dealt with

in the formal CISD continue to create major difficulties for a worker. Individual or group follow-ups might be effective. More than one session might be necessary and a formal referral might be in order. CISD has been adopted by business and industry, military organizations, and school systems, as well as its original target group of emergency services workers.

PREVENTING ORGANIZATIONAL BURNOUT

There is often a direct relationship between burnout in a workplace and a pervasive unwillingness to deal with the givens or realities of a situation. When unrealistically high expectations infiltrate the culture of a workplace and high stress levels become commonplace, the agency begins to show signs of organizational burnout: high absenteeism, lack of teamwork, tension among staff workers, decreased productivity, and, ultimately, high turnover. A group of disgruntled staff workers remain because they can't afford to leave yet. This should concern managers or supervisors of agencies, health care settings, corporations, schools, and virtually all other workplace settings. The director's expectations might not fit with what is feasible. Caseloads might be overburdening. Staff might be limited in size and training. The director might be asked to handle situations that the agency is not equipped to handle. These concerns, coupled with a lack of funds and the overabundance of paperwork, might be some of the problems that the director of an agency faces on a daily basis.

The following discussion is written for directors and supervisors. The importance of being able to assess realistically what you are able to do within the framework of a situation is essential to stress reduction. Problems of budget constraints, limited staff, overflowing paperwork, and large caseloads were mentioned in the previous paragraph. Given the situation, how will you allocate the budget that you do have? How will you administer the program with the existing staff? How can you work best within the existing facilities? What can you do to maintain a high level of staff morale? How can you foster an atmosphere conducive to productivity? In short, what can you and your staff do to minimize unwanted stress?

Will you spend your time as director being frustrated, wishing for a miracle that doesn't come, thereby creating additional anxiety within yourself and your staff? Or are you willing to use your energy to direct your agency along positive lines? How will you choose to arrange your life within the framework of what currently exists for you, your task, and those with whom you work at the moment? How you choose to invest your energy is a personal choice. It is a very important choice for your health and the health of your facility. The choice represents an opportunity for you to deal with stress reduction in your own life. It is also interesting to note the paradox that might be operating in these situations: The degree to which you exercise your choice to reduce stress in your life is the same degree to which some of your hopes for the future may be more nearly attainable.

The following suggestions are directed to managers and supervisors. The list is not intended to be exhaustive. We present this universal formula with the hope that you will tailor it to your particular environment. Let this be a catalyst for planning creatively, exploring options, and being innovative. Enjoy the process and the results.

Dr. Leviton's 50 Steps to Pro-Active Management for Reducing Stress in the Work Place

1. Be clear in preparing a job description.
   a. What are the objectives?
   b. Who has the background and training needed?
   c. What is the time frame of employment? Is the job temporary or permanent?
   d. How much time and money is involved?
2. Be clear in the interview with the prospective staff person.
   a. What the objectives of the job are.
   b. Whose background, training, experience and skills would indicate a suitable match for the position.
   c. When does the job start? Is the job temporary or permanent? What are the hours? Is flex time an option? Is there much overtime required? Are there evening or weekend meetings, travel assignments? How often do these occur? Are there sick days, holidays, vacation days?
   d. How much is the salary or compensation package? What benefits are included? When and how is payment made? Whether the workplace is a small agency or a large corporation, private or nonprofit, the prospective employee should be given complete, accurate, and reliable information

during the interview. Lack of clarity up front results in heightened stress later on.

    e. What are the supervisor's expectations? What are the agency's values and philosophy?

3. Be clear in delegating responsibility.
   a. What are the objectives of the assignment?
   b. With whom does the employee interface, report, and check?
   c. When are meetings held, reports due, memos circulated, and deadlines handled?
   d. How is information to be handled?
   e. How this job fits in the larger operation of the agency is important to the staff person.
4. Be clear in assigning tasks.
5. Be realistic in assigning responsibility.
   a. Is the time being allotted too little, too much, or accurate?
   b. Is the talent available? Who is the right person for the job?
   c. Are the current resources of personnel and money adequate for the job? If not, adjust as necessary. Set up for success, not for failure.
6. Be realistic in expectations of self and staff.
7. See the big picture. Every decision has an impact and a consequence.
8. Respond. Don't react.
9. Plan and then act.
10. Be consistent. Don't keep changing the rules. When employees are unclear about policy and function, their level of stress and anxiety escalates. Feeling out of structure without a mechanism for relief potentially results in a crisis situation.
11. Be reliable. Act reliably. Ensure that your actions match your words.
12. Create an environment that is orderly and efficient.
13. Be explicit in setting policy.
14. Provide support, structure, and information to your staff.
15. Encourage and place a value on staff creativity and innovation.
16. Communicate in a timely, appropriate, accurate manner.
17. Be accessible. When and how can you be reached?
18. Meet your employees and call them by name.

19. Take frequent field trips through your facility.
20. Be aware of your surroundings. You will gain valuable information about how things are going by using your sensing mechanisms.
21. Encourage input from your staff. It is all right not to have all the answers. Involving staff members increases their job satisfaction, commitment, and dedication to both the company and the job.
22. Give direction as needed and as appropriate.
23. Give feedback on a timely schedule.
24. Be fair. Act fairly despite personal biases.
25. Encourage professional development.
26. Create a safe environment. This includes both physical and emotional safety. Be clear that harassment of any nature will not be tolerated. Take necessary actions immediately if violations of the policy occur.
27. Create a supportive or nondefensive climate.
28. Identify potential stressors in your work environment.
29. Recognize symptoms of stress in yourself and in your staff.
30. Be aware of the relationship of unmanaged stress and crisis.
31. Understand the relationship of stress/crisis/burnout.
32. Decide how to respond to the stress that you are experiencing, the signs of stress that the staff member is exhibiting, and the potential stressors that you observed. Use what you have learned from earlier chapters in this book.
33. Recognize the cost of burnout to your agency.
34. Recognize the benefit to your organization of effective intervention.
35. Accept personal responsibility for your feelings and your behavior.
36. Allow your feelings to be what they are.
37. Separate your feelings from your behavior. You cannot always voluntarily change your feelings, but you can always voluntarily change your behavior.
38. Be realistic about the givens of your world. Work within the reality of "what is" today. Consider the implications such a realistic approach has for you and your employees.
39. Realistically assess what you are able to do in your particular situation.
40. Set realistic goals in all areas of your life.

41. Get sufficient rest and sleep.
42. Eliminate stressor foods from your diet. Nutritional stress can be as debilitating as emotional stress.
43. Schedule time on your calendar for fun. Allow time each day to experience good feelings.
44. Schedule time each week on your calendar for dreaming, thinking, wandering, exploring, planning, and being in touch with your dreams.
45. Encourage peer networks of support among employees.
46. Teach conflict resolution skills to your staff.
47. Recognize that evaluation of employee performance should be a continuous process rather than an occasional event.
     a. Discuss the evaluation procedure in advance with the supervisee.
     b. Encourage the supervisee to do a self-evaluation.
     c. Keep the focus of the evaluation on the supervisee's work performance.
     d. Review both strengths and weaknesses, growth and stagnation. Be fair and clear.
     e. Include an analysis of why certain behaviors and procedures are effective and why others are not.
     f. Focus on modifiable aspects of the supervisee's performance.
     g. Formulate the evaluations with some consistency. Apply the same standards in the same way to all of the supervisees who have approximately the same education and experience.
48. Recognize the necessity of humor in the work place.
49. Be aware that you set the climate for your organization.
50. Remember that most employees would like to feel a sense of commitment, challenge, and some control in their assignments.

CHILDREN'S REACTIONS TO CRISIS

TIPS FOR TEACHERS IN TIMES OF CRISIS

Taking Care of Yourself and Other School Staff

As teachers or school personnel, you are often in the "front lines" when dealing with children's reactions to crisis. You also need to consider your own crisis-related stress. It is extremely important to recognize that you, too, are under particular stress and vulnerable to "burnout."

Burnout reactions include the following:

- Depression, irritability, anxiety, overexcitability, excessive rage, and other similar reactions
- Physical exhaustion, loss of energy, gastrointestinal distress, appetite disturbances, hypochondria, sleep disorders, and tremors
- Hyperactivity, excessive fatigue, inability to express yourself verbally or in writing
- Slowness of thought, inability to make decisions, loss of objectivity in evaluating your own functioning, and external confusion
- Blaming the children, coldly responding to children's needs, withdrawing

It is important to recognize the symptoms and find ways to relieve the stress. You and others around you can form a support system by allowing each person to vent his or her experiences. Time might be set aside in staff meetings to discuss your own responses to the crisis as well as to share ideas on dealing with and assisting students.

Teaching is a highly stressful job under the best of circumstances. Dealing with your own responses to a crisis in addition to your students' reactions could easily feel overwhelming at times. Recognizing this fact and taking care of yourself and other school staff can help keep the stress at a manageable level.

GENERAL REACTIONS OF CHILDREN TO CRISIS

Although many feelings and reactions are shared by people of all ages in response to the direct or indirect effects of crisis, meeting the needs of children requires special attention.

Typical reactions of children, regardless of age, include the following:

- Fears stemming from the crisis extending to their home or neighborhood
- Loss of interest in school
- Regressive behavior
- Sleep disturbances and night terrors
- Fears of events that may be associated with the crisis situation, such as airplane sounds or loud noises

REACTIONS OF SPECIFIC AGE GROUPS

Children of different age groups tend to react in unique ways to the stress caused by crises and their consequences. The following typical reactions to stress are summarized for each age group and are followed by suggested responses.

Preschool (Ages 1–5)

Typical reactions to stress include the following:

- Thumb-sucking
- Bed-wetting
- Fear of the dark or of animals
- Clinging to parents
- Night terrors
- Loss of bladder or bowel control or constipation
- Speech difficulties
- Loss of or increase in appetite

- Fear of being left alone
- Immobility

Children in this age group are particularly vulnerable to disruption of their previously secure world. Because they lack the verbal and conceptual skills necessary to cope effectively with sudden stress by themselves, they look to family members for comfort. These children are often strongly affected by the reactions of parents and other family members.

Abandonment is a major fear in this age group. Children who have lost family members (or even pets or toys) because of circumstances either related or unrelated to the crisis will need special reassurance.

We recommend the following responses to help children integrate their experiences and reestablish a sense of security and mastery:

- Encourage expression through play reenactment where appropriate.
- Provide verbal reassurance and physical comforting.
- Give the child frequent attention.
- Encourage the child's expression of feelings and concerns regarding the loss, temporary or permanent, of family members, pets, toys, or friends.
- Provide comforting bedtime routines.
- Allow the child to sleep in the same room with the parent. Make it clear to the child that this is only for a limited period.

Early Childhood (Ages 5–11)

Common reactions to stress in this age group include the following:

- Irritability
- Whining
- Clinging
- Aggressive behavior at home or at school
- Overt competition with younger siblings for parent's attention
- Night terrors, nightmares, or fear of darkness
- School avoidance
- Loss of interest and poor concentration in school
- Fear of personal harm
- Confusion
- Fear of abandonment
- Generalized anxiety

Fear of loss is particularly difficult for these children to handle, and regressive behavior is most typical of this age group.

We recommend the following responses:

- Patience and tolerance.
- Play sessions with adults and peers where affective reactions can be openly discussed.
- Discussions with adults and peers about frightening, anxiety-producing aspects of events and about appropriate behavior to manage the child's concerns and the stress.
- Relaxation of expectations at school or at home. It should be made clear to the child that this relaxation is temporary and that the normal routine will be resumed after a suitable period.
- Opportunities for structured, but not unusually demanding, chores and responsibilities at home.
- Maintenance of a familiar routine as much as possible and as soon as possible.

Preadolescent (Ages 11–14)

The following are common reactions to stress for this age group:

- Sleep disturbances
- Appetite disturbance
- Rebellion in the home
- Refusal to do chores
- School problems, such as fighting, withdrawal, loss of interest, and attention-seeking behavior
- Physical problems, such as headaches, vague aches and pains, skin eruptions, bowel problems, and psychosomatic complaints
- Loss of interest in peer social activities
- Fear of personal harm
- Fear of impending loss of family members, friends, or home
- Anger
- Denial
- Generalized anxiety

Peer reactions are especially significant in preadolescence. These children need to feel that their fears are both appropriate and shared by others. Responses should be aimed at lessening tensions, anxieties, and possible guilt feelings.

We recommend the following responses:

- Group activities geared toward the resumption of routines
- Involvement with same-age group activity
- Group discussions geared toward examining feelings about the crisis and appropriate behavior to manage the concerns and the stress
- Structured, but undemanding, responsibilities
- Temporarily relaxed expectations of performance at school and at home
- Additional individual attention and consideration

Adolescent (Ages 14–18)

Common reactions in this age group include the following:

- Psychosomatic symptoms, such as rashes, bowel problems, and asthma
- Headaches and tension
- Appetite and sleep disturbances
- Hypochondriasis
- Amenorrhea or dysmenorrhea
- Agitation or decrease in energy level
- Apathy
- Decline in interest in the opposite sex
- Irresponsible behavior, delinquent behavior, or both
- Decline in emancipatory struggles over parental control
- Poor concentration
- Guilt
- Fear of loss
- Anger at the perceived unfairness of a crisis occurring in their lives
- Tendency to blame others for negative events that befall them

Most of the activities and interests of adolescents are focused in their own age-group peers. Adolescents tend to be especially distressed by the disruption of their peer-group activities and by their lack of access to full adult responsibilities in community efforts.

We recommend the following responses:

- Encourage participation in the community and in individual responses, such as letter writing.

- Encourage discussion of feelings, concerns, and shared information with peers and extrafamily significant others.
- Temporarily reduce expectations for specific levels of both school and general performance, depending on individual reactions.
- Encourage, but do not insist upon, discussions of crisis-induced fears within the family setting.

WHEN TO REFER CHILDREN TO MENTAL HEALTH PROFESSIONALS

A wide range of normal reactions surround crisis. Usually the reactions can be dealt with by support at home and at school, but this is not always the case. Sometimes a teacher needs to recommend professional help. In making such a referral, it is important to stress that it is not a sign of the parents' failure if they find they cannot help their child by themselves. It is also important to note that early action will help the child return to normal functioning and avoid more severe problems later.

Students who have lost family members or friends, either temporarily or permanently, or feel that they were in extreme danger are at special risk. Those who have been involved in individual or family crises in addition to the crisis they are currently experiencing might have more difficulty dealing with the additional stress. Counseling may be recommended as a preventive measure when these circumstances are known to exist.

Referral is recommended when symptoms that are considered normal reactions persist for several months or disrupt the student's social, mental, or physical functioning.

Referral for Preschool and Elementary School Children

Consider referring the family for professional help if the children react in these ways:

- Seem excessively withdrawn and depressed
- Do not respond to special attention and attempts to draw them out

Referral for Junior and Senior High School Children

Consider referral to a mental health professional if students react in the following ways:

- Are disoriented; for example, are unable to give their own name and address or the date
- Complain of significant memory gaps
- Are despondent and show agitation, restlessness, and pacing
- Are severely depressed and withdrawn
- Mutilate themselves
- Use drugs or alcohol excessively
- Are unable to care for themselves in such areas as eating, drinking, bathing, and dressing
- Repeat ritualistic acts
- Experience hallucinations, such as hearing voices or seeing visions
- State that their body feels "unreal" and express the concern that they are "going crazy"
- Are excessively preoccupied with one idea or thought
- Have the delusion that someone or something is out to get them and their family
- Are afraid they will commit suicide or kill another person
- Are unable to make simple decisions or carry out everyday functions
- Show extremely pressured speech or talk overflow
- Exhibit chronic disruptive behavior
- Make self-destructive decisions

CLASSROOM ACTIVITIES

Creative classroom activities help teachers seeking ways to deal with the stress and tension a crisis and its consequences create in students. The following activities are vehicles for expression and discussion for students and are important steps in helping children handle the stress they are experiencing. You can use these activities to stimulate your own ideas and adapt them to meet both your students' needs and your teaching style.

Preschool Activities

1. Make available some toys that encourage play enactment of the child's concerns. Such toys might include airplanes, helicopters, toy police officers, toy soldiers, rescue trucks, ambulances, building blocks, puppets, or dolls. Playing with these toys allows the child to ventilate feelings about what is occurring or has already occurred.

2. Children need lots of physical contact during times of stress to help them reestablish ego boundaries and a sense of security. Introduce games that involve physical toughening among children within a structure. Examples include "Ring around the Rosy," "London Bridge," and "Duck, Duck, Goose."

3. Provide extra amounts of drinks and finger foods in small portions. This is a concrete way of supplying the emotional and physical nourishment children need in times of stress. Oral satisfaction is especially necessary because children tend to revert to more regressive behavior in response to feeling that their survival or security is threatened.

4. Have the children make a mural on butcher paper, using topics related to what is happening in the world and in their community. This is recommended for small groups, with discussion afterwards facilitated by the teacher or other skilled adult.

5. Have the children draw individual pictures about the crisis situation and then discuss the pictures in small groups. This activity allows children to vent their experiences and to discover that others share their fears.

6. Make a group collage, and discuss what the collage represents, how it was made, and the feelings it evokes.

Elementary School Activities

1. For younger children, make toys available that encourage play to express concerns, fears, and observations. These toys might include ambulances, planes, tanks, helicopters, toy police officers, rescue vehicles, toy soldiers, building blocks, and dolls. Play with puppets can provide ways for older children, as well as younger children, to ventilate their feelings.

2. Help or encourage the children to develop skits or puppet shows about what happened during the crisis. Encourage

them to include anything positive about the experience as well as frightening or disconcerting aspects.

3. Have the children create short stories about the crisis and how it was managed. These stories can be either written or dictated to an adult, depending on the age of the child.

4. Have the children draw pictures and discuss them in relation to the crisis. It is important that the group discussion end on a positive note if at all possible. Mastery and having a vehicle for expressing concerns are equally important.

5. Stimulate group discussion about crisis and its consequences by showing your own feelings or fears. It is very important to legitimize children's feelings and to help children feel less isolated. It is equally important to give them a sense of structure, balance, and control over their own activities and life.

6. Have the children brainstorm their own ways of handling their concerns. Encourage them to discuss the results with their parents.

7. Encourage class activities in which the children can organize and build projects, such as scrapbooks, to give them a sense of mastery and ability to organize what seems chaotic and confusing.

8. Encourage the children to talk about their own feelings about the crisis.

9. Have children brainstorm ways to be supportive of the family after the death of a classmate or a family's loss of a home because of fire or natural disaster. Have the students take steps to follow up on their plan.

Junior and Senior High School Activities

1. Conduct a group discussion of the students' experiences concerning the crisis situation and the events surrounding it. This is particularly important to adolescents because they need the opportunity to vent as well as to normalize the extreme emotions that arise in them. A good way to stimulate such a discussion is for you to share your personal reactions. The students might need considerable reassurance that even extreme emotions and "crazy" thoughts are normal under these circumstances. It is important to end such discussions on a positive note. Such discussion is appropriate for any

course of study because it can hasten a return to more normal functioning.

2. Conduct a class discussion or support a class project on how students might involve themselves in activities related to managing the crisis. This might include support groups, rallies, and assistance to family members. It is important to help students develop concrete, realistic ways to assist or to be involved. This helps them to overcome the feelings of helplessness, frustration, and guilt common to these situations.

3. Introduce classroom activities that relate the crisis and its consequences to course study. This can be an effective way to help students integrate their own experiences or observations while providing specific learning experiences. In performing these activities, it is very important to allow time for the students to discuss feelings stimulated by the projects or the issues covered.

The following suggestions could be carried out within specific courses. Teachers are encouraged to expand these suggestions to fit the students' needs and the teacher's individual style.

Journalism Have the students write stories that cover different aspects of the crisis. These might include stories about community and personal impact, human interest, and ecological impact. You might also discuss issues such as accurate reporting, censorship, and sensationalism, and students could compile the stories into a special publication.

Science Discuss the scientific aspects of the crisis, such as weapons and their destructive power, research, impact of the weather, environmental impact, and impact on the school. Suggest a project about stress involving the physiological responses to stress and methods of dealing with it.

English Composition Have the students write about their own experiences, or those of persons close to them, regarding the crisis and the problems associated with it. You might discuss composition issues, such as the problems that arise in conveying heavy emotional tone without being overly dramatic.

Literature Have students report on crises that have occurred in mythology or that appear in American and British fiction and poetry.

Psychology Have the students apply what they have learned in the course to the emotions, behaviors, and stress reactions they felt or observed in response to the crisis. Cover posttraumatic stress syndrome as appropriate. Present a guest speaker from the mental health profession who may be involved in working with families affected by the crisis or with support groups. Have students discuss, from their own experience, what has helped them most in dealing with crisis-related stress. Have the students develop a mental health education brochure in which they discuss emotional and behavioral reactions to crisis and the things that are helpful in coping. Have students conduct a survey among their parents and friends about how the crisis affected each of them and how they reacted psychologically.

Peer Counseling Provide special information about common responses to the onset of the crisis and the consequences associated with it. Encourage the students to help each other integrate their own experiences.

Health Discuss emotional reactions to crisis and the importance of taking care of one's own emotional and physical well-being. Discuss health implications of crisis, including food, water, physical and mental wounds, exposure to the elements, and other health precautions and safety measures. Discuss the effects of adrenaline on the body during stress and danger. A public health or mental health professional could be invited to speak to the class. Maintaining health, from the viewpoints of all those involved in or affected by the crisis, might be a valuable discussion topic.

Art Have the students portray the crisis and their concerns about it in various art media. Students can do this individually or as a group.

Speech and Drama Have the students portray the emotions, feelings, and stresses that have arisen in response to the crisis and the effects of the crisis on each of them. Ask students to develop a skit or play on some aspect of the crisis. Stage a debate about whether women or men are better prepared psychologically to handle the stress of a crisis such as the one the students experienced.

Mathematics Have the class solve mathematical problems related to the impact of the crisis.

Civics and Government Study governmental agencies responsible either directly or indirectly for causing or supporting the crisis and their

AGE-SPECIFIC REACTIONS OF CHILDREN AFFECTED BY CRISIS AND ITS CONSEQUENCES

Preschoolers	Elementary School Children	Preadolescents/ Adolescents
Crying	Headaches/physical complaints	Headaches/physical complaints
Thumb-sucking	Depression	Depression
Loss of bowel control	Fears about safety	Confusion
Fears of being left alone and of strangers	Confusion	Poor performance
Irritability	Inability to concentrate	Aggressive behavior
Confusion	Poor performance	Withdrawal
Clinging	Fighting	Isolation
Immobility	Withdrawal from peers	

AGE-SPECIFIC INTERVENTIONS FOR CHILDREN REACTING TO CRISIS

Preschoolers	Elementary School Children	Preadolescents/ Adolescents
Draw a picture	Draw a picture	Stories and essays
Tell a story	Tell a story	Books on effects of crisis
Coloring books	Books on effects of crisis	Create a play about the crisis
Books on effects of crisis	Create a game	School project/ natural sciences
Doll, toy play	Create a play	School project/ social sciences
Group games	School study project	School health project
Talks about safety	Materials about personal and family safety	Materials about personal and family safety and community protection

response to the crisis. Discuss how these agencies work and the political implications and impact of each agency. Examine various community systems and how the stress of the crisis has affected them. Have the students invite a local government official to class to discuss how the crisis has affected the community. Encourage the students to become aware of current and pending legislation relating to the crisis, should such legislation exist, and the implications of this legislation on them and on their families.

History Have the students report on crises that have occurred both around the world and in the geographical location of the current crisis. What lessons can and have been learned that could benefit us and our communities in the future?

CHAPTER

8

HOT-LINE WORKERS

The immediacy of crisis situations dictates the need for immediate service delivery. Hot-line services are as close as the telephone and are usually available 24 hours a day, seven days a week. As a rule, the caller can obtain assistance without the need for self-identification.

Hot-line work is difficult. It requires that the intervener compensate for the inability to see the caller's appearance, behavior, and body language as the caller speaks or listens. The intervener must remain focused and free of distractions that could impede his or her ability to listen to the caller. We recommend the following "do's" and "don'ts" for hot-line workers.

Do's

DO establish a feeling of trust, support, and confidence.

DO allow the caller to speak freely and to ventilate feelings.

DO listen carefully, not only to what is being said, but also to what is not being said.

DO encourage callers to tell you what is troubling them.

DO accept callers' right to feel as they do. The way they see the world at this time in their life is real for them.

DO listen attentively and reflect feelings.

DO be honest. If you do not know an answer or cannot provide the information requested, say so.

DO ask for feedback to find out if you are on the right track.

DO be realistic.

80

DO ask what the caller is doing currently to manage the particular discomfort the caller is experiencing.

DO ask how the caller has managed traumatic events in the past.

DO help the caller draw from past successes in managing current personal crises.

DO be alert for opportunities to reinforce the caller's strengths and positive qualities.

DO build a sense of structure that the caller can relate to.

DO help callers identify areas in their personal life over which they can assert control. Stress the need to devote energy to these areas rather than to areas over which they have no control.

DO have updated, immediately available referral resources.

DO get in touch and stay in touch with yourself and what you, as the hot-line worker, are feeling.

DO separate your needs, concerns, and values from the caller's. Respond to what the caller needs.

DO debrief with a fellow hot-line worker as needed.

DO trust yourself to ask effective questions, to offer appropriate options, and to know when to stop.

DO remember that your job is to listen, empathize, and help set some sense of structure for the caller, who might feel out of control.

DO remember that hot-line work is stressful. Take time to care for yourself as you care for others.

DO maintain boundaries. Avoid using the situation to resolve a similar or current crisis in your own life.

DON'TS

DON'T offer any service you cannot provide.

DON'T agree or disagree with callers. The way they see the world at this time is real to them.

DON'T interrupt callers while they are talking unless absolutely necessary. If you need more details, wait until the caller is finished, and then go back and ask for the needed information.

DON'T argue with a caller.

DON'T be afraid of silence. Give the caller time to think and feel.

DON'T assume anything. Ask for clarification if you are
     concerned about the caller's physical and emotional safety.
DON'T allow the caller's anger or hostility to intimidate you.
DON'T push your value system on the caller.
DON'T push your religious beliefs on the caller.
DON'T be afraid to admit that a caller might need further help
     that you cannot provide. Refer as necessary and as appropriate.
DON'T allow callers to concentrate only on the negative aspects
     of their situation. Help them develop options.
DON'T show excessive pity or sympathy.
DON'T use the situation for a catharsis about a similar or parallel
     loss or crisis in your own life. Maintain boundaries.

TWENTY STEPS FOR HANDLING THE DIFFICULT CALLER

As hot-line workers and phone counselors, our job is to assist, to answer,
perhaps to counsel, and certainly to help those who call. Occasionally
the caller is upset to the point of belligerency either because of the
emotional trauma suffered or because of extreme anger experienced for
some other reason. Callers in this situation could become abusive to the
hot-line worker and, if not checked appropriately, will contaminate all
attempts to be helpful.

     The following are suggested as a nonexhaustive guide to handling
difficult and abusive calls and callers.

1. Stop talking.
2. Take a deep breath.
3. Listen for the caller's real message.
4. If possible, legitimize the caller's anger.
5. Listen carefully for clues as to what is really going on with the
    caller.
6. Reduce the volume of your own voice when speaking. Your
    action might cause the callers to lower their voices also, or at
    least to stop talking so they can hear what you are saying.
7. Do not argue with the caller or become defensive. The
    caller's remarks or abuse is usually not intended for you per-
    sonally. The caller would probably make the same remarks to
    whomever answered the phone.
8. Clarify your role with the caller.

9. Refuse to be verbally abused by the caller: "I want to listen to what you are saying, but I won't listen to insults, threats, or personal attacks on me."

10. State the ground rules for your being able to provide assistance to the caller. These include the caller's refraining from abusive talk.

11. Keep your responses clear and simple.

12. Once you have stated the ground rules, let the caller decide whether or not he or she wishes to continue the conversation. Continue with the conversation only if the caller agrees to abide by the ground rules.

13. Avoid being judgmental of anything the caller says. Remember, the way the caller sees the world is accurate for that caller.

14. Remember: Do not take personally any abusive remarks the caller makes to you.

15. Ask for and obtain a clear commitment from the caller that he or she will continue the conversation without abusive talk and according to the agreed-upon ground rules.

16. Continue to repeat your willingness to keep trying to assist the caller, and repeat the ground rules for continuing.

17. Always be aware of, and continue to evaluate, the caller's actual threat potential to you.

18. If all else fails in your attempt to deal with the caller's abusive or otherwise difficult behavior, terminate the call.

19. Debrief immediately after a difficult or abusive phone call.

20. *Remember: You are the professional and you are in control.*

FAMILY CRISIS

Excessive stress and tension, usually resulting from multiple or major changes in a person's life, are often the basis of most crisis situations. Because family members do not operate in a vacuum, one person's crisis often becomes a crisis for the family. Major sources of personal crises include illness, financial problems, business problems, job promotions or demotions, problems with one's children, layoffs, maintenance of a career or the beginning of a new one, adoption or birth of children, abortion, pending marriages, separations and divorces, blending of stepfamilies, and severe injuries and deaths in the family. These events can also be a source of crisis for all the members of a family.

Most crises have a primary victim, but they also touch those who are affected through the primary victim. These secondary victims are usually significant others of the person experiencing the crisis. In rapes, suicide, battering, incest, drug abuse, family disputes, and natural disasters, the intensity of the trauma, the emotional upheaval, and the difficulty in adjustment relating to the event can be as severe for the significant others as for the primary victim. Secondary victims often experience their own crisis as they try to fit what has happened into life as they see it. For example, a rape victim's parents, spouse, or boyfriend, or the children who witnessed the rape, might experience their own crisis with an intensity equal to, or even greater than, that of the primary victim. Guidelines and procedures for managing crisis situations with primary victims must be applied in a similar manner to significant others. Unfortunately, the intervener often overlooks this task.

Children may have it worst of all. Generally they lack even the limited understanding adults possess. Children's reality is often formed by fantasy, partial truths, and an immature ability to discern what is happening around them.

THIRTY STEPS FOR HANDLING FAMILY CRISES

1. Pull together as a family by establishing a sense of purpose.
2. Allow your feelings to be whatever they are; avoid berating yourself or discounting your feelings or those of your children.
3. Let your children talk with you about their fears, concerns, confusion, anger, sadness, and problems.
4. Talk in words your children can understand. Avoid euphemisms.
5. Allow your children to see your grief, and be honest with them about your feelings. Avoid as much gore as possible in your expressions.
6. Don't expect your children to resolve your grief.
7. Reassure children that they are safe and will be taken care of.
8. Don't be afraid to say that you do not know the answers to your children's questions. Your honesty may make it easier for them to tolerate the ambiguity in their own minds.
9. If a death occurs, share with your children in terms that they can understand, and avoid euphemisms.
10. Remember that children often take their lead for their own behavior from their parents. Children will watch and learn how you handle crises.
11. Children will look to you for structure, guidance, limits, and support. Give these things to them.
12. Ask your children what they need from you. Maybe they need a hug, time to talk, play time with you, or straight talk. Children of different ages will need different things at different times. Adapt your actions to your children's ages and levels of maturity.
13. Identify areas of concern in your life over which you have control, and exercise that control.
14. Have realistic expectations of yourself and your children to minimize stress.
15. Be realistic about each child's role in the family.

16. Continue projects that you have already begun.
17. Create a routine for yourself, and stick with it.
18. Maintain your personal health and hygiene.
19. Plan outings and activities with friends. This mutual support can be helpful.
20. Set boundaries with your children. Hear their feelings, and understand the behavior that might result from these feelings. Establish limits to provide stability, structure, and continuity. Don't overdo it by being too strict or too lenient.
21. Observe changes in your children's behavior, attitudes, and expressions. Pay attention to both verbal and nonverbal behavior. Be prepared to respond as appropriate.
22. Use support groups as necessary for your children and for yourself. Participate separately or together with your children, as appropriate.
23. Obtain professional help for yourself and your children as needed. Sometimes counseling in conjunction with support groups offers maximum benefit.
24. Find something to laugh about every day. Use laughter as a stress manager and reducer.
25. Walk or exercise regularly, and include sufficient rest and relaxation in your schedule.
26. Both for yourself and for your children, maintain the continuity of the familiar. This includes schedules, school attendance, friendships, TV programs, and regular activities.
27. Listen.
28. Hear.
29. Respond.
30. Don't lecture.

How Parents Can Help Their Children Cope with Crisis-Related Feelings

1. Talk with your child; provide simple, accurate answers to questions.
2. Talk with your child about your own feelings.
3. Listen to what your child says and how your child says it. Does the child display fear, anxiety, or insecurity? Repeating

your child's words can be very helpful. Use phrases such as "You are afraid that . . ." or "You wonder if. . . ." This helps both you and the child clarify feelings.

4. Reassure your child. For example, tell your child, "We are together. I care about you, and I will take care of you."

5. You may need to repeat information and reassurances to your child many times. Do not stop responding just because you told the child something once.

6. Hold your child. Provide comfort. Touching is important for children during crises.

7. Spend extra time putting your child to bed; talk and offer reassurance. Leave a night-light on if necessary.

8. Observe your child at play. Listen to what your child says, and watch how your child plays. Frequently, children express feelings of fear or anger while playing with dolls, toy trucks, or friends.

9. Provide play experiences to relieve tension. Work with Play-Doh, paint pictures, play in water, and the like. If children display a need to hit or kick, give them something safe, such as a pillow or a ball.

10. If your child has an especially meaningful toy or blanket, allow the child to rely on it somewhat more than usual.

11. If you need professional assistance, seek it early to maximize its benefits.

CRISIS, STRESS, AND HOLIDAY CELEBRATIONS

Thanksgiving, Christmas, Easter, Hanukkah, Passover, New Year's Day, birthdays, and anniversaries all come sooner than we expect. For many people, the prospect of the holidays and of family celebrations is filled with anguish and anxiety. And when these holidays and celebrations take place without that special loved one, they are much harder to get through. Holidays can be accompanied by the emotional battering of anticipatory stress followed by postholiday blues. It can take weeks to recover from the agony of unfulfilled expectations, the debt resulting from overspending to create the "perfect holiday," and the disappointment of rediscovering that family conflicts and losses remain unresolved despite the promises of holiday music and commercial messages.

Therapists know that holidays are times when patients and clients often turn away from the hard work they have been doing with their counselors and rely on the season, the holiday, or the celebration to do it for them. Loan officers know they will be deluged with requests from people who will "buy now and worry later."

During holiday seasons, loneliness, depression, alienation, stress, exacerbated personal problems and situations, financial problems, dissatisfaction, disappointment, lack of fulfillment, unrealized hopes, aging, loss, gain, fear, anxiety, terror, guilt, and unresolved worry plague many of us. Present perhaps all year long, tensions increase with the expectation that somehow, in some way, the holiday will make it "all better." The season itself does little or nothing to solve the problems in our lives. Yet many of us annually perpetuate the fantasy that this year it will be different. The responsibility for creating emotional comfort rests with the individual, not the season. Changing our belief from "the holiday will make it better" to "I will make it better" is the first major step in managing holiday stress and preventing postholiday letdown.

Twenty Steps for Avoiding Holiday Crisis

1. Be realistic in your expectations about holidays and celebrations. Keep the euphemisms about the holiday in balance, and accept things as they are at the moment. Remember that acceptance does not necessarily mean agreement.
2. Remember, it is not what the holiday does for us, but what we do with the holiday that makes the difference. Use these events to build family unity, strengthen the bonds between family members, and remember loved ones who are far away.
3. Recognize that you are responsible for your life and that nothing and no one can be responsible for you. Saying to yourself, "If only Bob were here, everything would be OK," merely sidesteps your getting on with your life as necessary.
4. Live year-round, and especially at this season, by the present realities, not by your fantasy of how you want things to be.
5. Look to yourself as the source of your well-being and happiness.
6. Spend realistically. Give realistically. Going into debt will not create a "perfect" holiday or celebration.
7. Put gift giving and tasks in perspective. Remember that people are more important than things and events.
8. Recognize your grown children as adults.

9. If necessary, remind your parents that you are an adult.

10. Clarify family expectations long before the holiday season. Communicate feelings, exchange ideas, discuss arrangements, and check schedules; include all family members as appropriate. Avoid assumptions.

11. If you are planning a visit with your parents, make your expectations clear. Let your parents know you intend to visit with friends outside the family. Alert your parents to arrangements you might be considering. Avoid assumptions about baby-sitting, sleeping arrangements, transportation, and so on. "Home for the holidays" can be either a nightmare or a lovely experience. Consideration, fairness, clarity, careful planning, and shared feelings help determine a visit's success.

12. Invite your parents to your home for the holiday.

13. Acknowledge and allow for the feelings you experience. What you feel is very real. Allow yourself to miss loved ones who are away, and allow your children to express their feelings. Remember it is all right to let your children see your feelings; it may help them learn more about handling theirs.

14. Share the work of holiday events. Assuming all the responsibility often results in victimhood.

15. Manage your time. Learn to say no when saying yes would be unrealistic.

16. Stick to regular diet and sleep routines as much as possible.

17. To avoid letdown, plan some interesting activities for after the holidays.

18. If you are in counseling, stay in counseling during the holiday season.

19. Learn to appreciate who and what you have rather than wishing you had someone or something else.

20. Enjoy this particular time of year, and this particular time of your life. It will never happen again.

GRIEF

THE GRIEF FACTOR IN CRISIS SITUATIONS

Every crisis situation involves an element of grief. Crisis involves loss, and loss often results in grief. A person grieves over the loss of anything felt to be important in his or her life. If the loss is so great that it totally tears apart the sufferer's sense of well-being, the person will experience crisis. If the loss is felt to be minor, the grieving process might be completed quickly with the person using his or her normal coping mechanisms.

It is important for the intervener to understand that three elements determine the effect of grief on an individual. These are the intensity of the emotions experienced as a result of the loss, the personal value attached to the loss, and the perceived long-term effects the loss will have on the person's life. As in every crisis situation, the significance of the loss is determined by the sufferer. Crisis is always in the eyes of the beholder. The way the victim currently perceives the world is the victim's reality. The intervener must recognize this principle to be effective and, thus, helpful to the sufferer. Consider the following statements made by crisis victims to the crisis intervener:

- "We moved into a brand-new beautiful home last month."
- "My daughter got married last week to a fine young man."
- "I retired yesterday."
- "My company was downsized. I lost my job."
- "My wallet was stolen."
- "My husband was granted sole custody of our kids."

- "My wife died recently."
- "My house was broken into yesterday."
- "I can't find the paper napkin." (The victim is 4 years old.)
- "I just found out that I have breast cancer."
- "My dog died this morning."

The first 3 situations might seem to evoke joyful, positive reactions. The final 8 situations might seem to evoke sad, negative reactions. Let's read again the statements made by the sufferer to the crisis intervener. Under each statement is an additional statement identifying the crisis. This information would have been brought out during the assessment phase of the intervention.

- "We moved into a brand new beautiful home last week."
  Crisis: I didn't want to leave my friends, my neighbors, my garden that I spent 8 years developing. I loved our lifestyle there. I just need to go back to my real home. That's where I was happy.
- "My daughter got married last week to a fine young man."
  Crisis: My little girl is gone. The family unit is disrupted. I've dreaded this, and now it's here.
- "I lost my job."
  Crisis: I worked at that company for 40 years. I was top dog there. Now I'm just another nobody.
- "My company downsized. I lost my job."
  Crisis: What am I going to do? In my culture, it isn't accepted for the woman to work and certainly not to earn more than the man. Who is going to respect me?
- "My wallet was stolen."
  Crisis: No, I wasn't physically harmed. What I cherished most was taken. I can't replace my pictures.
- "My husband was granted sole custody of our kids."
  Crisis: My kids are going to think I didn't fight hard enough to get them. They're going to think I don't love them. That kills me. I'll never get over this loss.
- "My wife died recently."
  Crisis: I'm so lonely. I'm so lost. Nothing helps.
- "My house was broken into yesterday."
  Crisis: I feel violated.

- "I can't find the paper napkin."
  Crisis: My daddy drew my picture on it before the car killed him.
- "I just found out that I have breast cancer."
  Crisis: They are going to operate. I'm losing part of my body. I might be losing my life.
- "My dog died this morning."
  Crisis: It's not really the dog. He was kind of a nuisance. It's that I can't handle another death, another loss.

What has become evident is that what the 11 situations share is the presence of grief at a personal level.

This is an excellent opportunity to underscore what was stated in Chapter 3 regarding communications. All communications contain three messages: a content message, a feeling message, and a meaning message. Had the intervener in the first three situations not been alert, he or she might only have heard the content message and assumed this was not a crisis situation. This would have closed down the communications and exacerbated the crisis.

1. Encourage and allow sufferers to express emotions without your judging them.

MR. JONES: *I retired a month ago after 35 years at the same company.*
INTERVENER: *I see such sadness in your eyes.*
MR. JONES: *I can't stop crying. It's like my whole world just stopped. . . . I feel so ashamed because everybody keeps telling me how lucky I am now that I can do anything I want. I want to go back to being somebody . . . I want to feel important and alive! I'm just waiting to die.*

2. Let sufferers take the time necessary to express feelings before addressing options.

INTERVENER: *Mr. Smith, you said that no one understands what you're going through.*
MR. SMITH: *I've been offered a partnership in an aggressive, well-established firm.*
INTERVENER: *What does that offer mean to you?*

MR. SMITH: *A lot more pain. You see, I'll have to move to the West Coast.*

INTERVENER: *And what does that mean?*

MR. SMITH: *I just went through a bad divorce . . . I lost my wife, the house, a lot of things important to me. My parents live here now. This move means giving up more things and more people. . . . Financially, I can't afford not to go. . . . But I can't give up anything more.*

INTERVENER: *I hear how hard this decision is for you. There are lots of feelings about moving and giving things up that are important to you.*

3. Assure sufferers that their emotions are normal and acceptable.

MRS. BROWN: *My husband died six weeks ago. I don't think I want to go on anymore either.*

INTERVENER: *I'm sorry for your pain, Mrs. Brown. What do you need right now?*

MRS. BROWN: *You're the only one who has asked me that. Everybody else is so busy telling me what I should do and what I should feel. I have had to be brave so I wouldn't hurt anybody's feelings or worry my children. I'm about to crack up!*

INTERVENER: *It's hard to keep up appearances.*

MRS. BROWN: *Please, just let me be me for a little while. Just let me be me.*

INTERVENER: *Take your time. I'm here.*

4. Assure sufferers that they can live through a lonely, painful experience.

INTERVENER: *I hear the pain. I don't know exactly what you're experiencing, but I know you are hurting a great deal. I know you can get through this.*

5. Let sufferers talk about feelings of guilt that might be associated with the crisis. Accept the validity of the guilt feelings just as you do the validity of other feelings expressed.
6. Allow sufferers to express anger and resentment about the loss. Assure them that these feelings are normal.
7. Remain caring, interested, and nonjudgmental.

8. Reach out to sufferers in appropriate ways.
9. Reach out physically only with permission.

WHAT SUFFERERS MIGHT EXPERIENCE DURING THE GRIEF PROCESS

Feeling off balance
Dizziness
Feeling uncoordinated
Erratic appetite
Disturbed sleep patterns
Feeling drugged without having taken drugs or medication
Feeling "out of sync" with one's own body
Irritability
Anger
Feeling disconnected from family, friends, and associates
Feeling disoriented
Rage from deep within one's own body
Feeling as though one is "falling apart" physically and emotionally
Feeling out of control
Deep sadness
Hopelessness
Feeling unwilling and/or incapable of making decisions
Feeling that nothing has meaning and nothing matters
Feeling frozen in time and space
Feeling that all activity, no matter how limited, is too much effort
Confusion
Embarrassment about feelings
Guilt
An overwhelming sense of panic that nothing will ever feel right
    again
Feeling of spinning around but getting nowhere
Resentment that the loss has occurred
Relief that the ordeal leading to the final loss is over, and then
    guilt at feeling relieved
Feeling empty
Feeling numb
Feeling pushed down, buried, and very small

Turmoil associated with new or competing emotions
Ambivalence
Euphoria one moment and depression the next

SELF-INTERVENTION FOR SUFFERERS

Interveners should help sufferers to do the following:

1. Feel their own feelings. Let the feelings be whatever they are.
2. Avoid major changes that will require being uprooted physically or emotionally from loved ones, support systems, and that which is familiar and safe.
3. Put major decisions on hold.
4. Rely on the security of the familiar.
5. Set realistic expectations concerning work, home, chores, family obligations, and all other areas of life.
6. Seek out those people who are helpful and comforting and avoid, where possible, those who exacerbate the sufferer's discomfort. Being well-intentioned does not necessarily translate into helpful behavior.
7. Recognize that the death of a significant other creates a sense of helplessness in survivors. Sufferers should identify those areas of life over which they have control and exercise that control immediately.
8. Maintain a daily routine. Persons suffering from grief should get up, get dressed, get out, and get moving every morning. This helps give the sufferer a sense of purpose and direction.
9. Care for themselves as follows:
   a. If work schedules do not permit rest during the day, arrange a routine after or before work to allow for extra rest as needed.
   b. Take appropriate vitamins to supplement the diet and minimize stress.
   c. Exercise daily to relieve tension.
   d. Walk daily and allow the senses of touch, smell, feeling, hearing, and sight to be energizers.
10. Let the process of recovery take as long as it takes.
11. Discover and use personal strengths.

COPING WITH SEPARATION AND THE UNKNOWN

Interveners should help sufferers do the following:

1. Concentrate on the present.
2. Avoid trying to focus on the distant future.
3. Live for today.
4. Enjoy family and social relationships, and allow talk about thoughts and feelings as needed.
5. Finish projects previously started. If none are in progress, start a project and find enjoyment in it.
6. View each day as a victory.
7. Remember that each of us copes in different ways. People should find the best way by listening to their needs.
8. Accept personal responsibility for life as a way of helping oneself
9. Participate actively in daily routines.
10. Set realistic goals.
11. Reach out to others and let them know the sufferer's wants, needs, and concerns.
12. Accept responsibility for their own frames of mind.
13. Set the tone for others with whom they associate.
14. Work with family, friends, and co-workers to help build and maintain a sense of control, purpose, and hope.
15. Encourage honest, open communication.
16. Remember that there will be good times and bad times.
17. Focus on the good and never lose hope that more good times lie ahead.
18. Share thoughts and feelings only when they wish to.
19. Be aware that sometimes talking with others eases emotional weight.
20. Remember that talking to others can provide new insight into dealing with a specific problem or situation.
21. Remember that if they cannot talk to family or friends, perhaps a professionally trained counselor would be helpful.
22. Recognize that self-help groups and sharing of common concerns can aid in the healing process.
23. Remember that letting feelings out with others can be a great release.

24. Try to live each day as fully as possible.
25. Discover that some concerns can be eased with current information, emotional support, knowledge, faith, and love.
26. Know that a decision to make the most of life, even in the face of separation, can help them.
27. Recognize that communication with loved ones will keep the sufferer in touch with significant others and with the world around them.
28. Live with a sense of purpose and the hope that good relationships will continue and that family, friends, and key support persons will be available to provide needed support.
29. Choose small goals and constructive ways to use time.
30. Ask "What is important to me right now?" and "What do I cherish?"
31. Think of the needs of other families, their own family, friends, and others who are important.
32. Keep a daily journal of feelings, thoughts, and experiences.
33. Direct personal energy into living each day as it comes and make each day count by what they put into it.
34. Try to live as normally as possible.
35. Keep close at hand things that have always provided enjoyment, such as photos, art, music, magazines, and books.
36. Surround themselves with familiar things.
37. Keep up with local and national news.
38. Ask others to go out for a meal or movie or to just drop by for a visit.
39. Recognize that on some days the sufferer may want to be left alone and that this is OK.
40. Maintain self-respect even though it may sometimes seem difficult.

THE CRISIS REVISITED: COPING WITH THE AFTERMATH

For many, a crisis stirs painful memories of previous crises. Thus, crisis victims are required to deal with feelings that either were never resolved or were thought to be resolved. The emotional wounds seem fresh, and the bleeding recurs. The anniversary date of a crisis can be difficult. People often feel a sense of free-floating anxiety at this time.

The following are some reactions common to people who experience traumatic stress as a result of a tragic incident. You may have these reactions if you have survived or witnessed a traumatic event. These reactions vary in intensity and duration and can occur whether or not you are physically injured. Although these thoughts, feelings, and behaviors can be very upsetting, it is important to remember that they are normal reactions to abnormal situations.

Thoughts

- Repeated thoughts or memories of the event
- Recurring dreams or nightmares
- Being caught off guard by a person, place, or event that reminds you of the original event
- Reconstructing the event in your mind in an effort to regain a sense of control
- Trouble concentrating or remembering things
- Questioning your view of the world or your spiritual beliefs
- Ruminating over the "what ifs" and "if only's" of the circumstances surrounding the event

Feelings

- Feeling pervasive fear
- Feeling emotionally numb or withdrawn
- Lacking enjoyment in everyday activities
- Feeling depressed
- Distrusting others
- Feeling anger, including a desire for revenge or vengeance

Behaviors

- Being extremely alert or startling easily
- Being overprotective of your own and your family's safety
- Being surprised by the somatic responses to death

LEGAL IMPLICATIONS OF CRISIS INTERVENTION[1]

Although Crisis Intervention and the intervener's function is not about the legalities involved, one should at least consider how these legalities relate to intervention. We live in a litigious society, where self-responsibility is often lacking and lawsuits are often the remedy. Lawsuits can be filed against anyone, at almost any time and for almost any reason if a plaintiff feels that a personal wrong or injury has been caused. Generally such claims are brought under civil or tort law rather than under criminal law. That is, civil offenses or torts have been committed against individuals rather than against the state.

Nothing said here can completely prevent such action or insulate the intervener from all exposure. However, some guidelines, procedures, and areas of awareness can ease the potential legal burden of the intervener and allow everyone to get on with the real job—effective assistance to those in crisis.

Not all areas of concern to interveners will be dealt with extensively in this chapter. All interveners, however, should be familiar with the following issues and how the laws regarding these issues apply to them.

Interveners may need to do individual research to ascertain the information they need. For that purpose legal references are provided at the end of this chapter. The following are some issues that may apply to interveners:

Negligence
Informed consent
Confidentiality

---

[1]Nothing stated in this chapter should be construed in any way to be legally definitive or to replace your own research into the laws of your state and city. Nor should you take this information as legal advice or as negation of the importance of seeking competent counsel from a licensed attorney.

Exceptions to confidentiality
Duty to warn
Record keeping
Right to privacy
Right to refuse intervention
Good Samaritan laws
Standards of care
Abandonment
Consent to intervention
Actual consent
Implied consent

To work effectively in the Crisis Intervention field, interveners must recognize that they are bound by the laws of society and that, even under extreme circumstances, such proscriptions cannot be ignored without consequence. Good Samaritan laws generally protect those whose intent is to assist others in times of crisis. Such assistance must always be reasonable and prudent and must be based on the level and kind of training the intervener has received and now applies. To such standards of care we must adhere.

For example, the Good Samaritan Law of the State of Texas (Chapter 74 of the Civil Practice and Remedies Code, 2000) states that

(a) A person who in good faith administers emergency care, including using an automated external defibrillator at the scene of an emergency but not in a hospital or other health care facility or means of medical support is not liable in civil damages for an act performed during the emergency unless the act is willfully or wantonly negligent.
(b) This section does not apply to care administered:
   (1) for or in expectation of remuneration; or
   (2) by a person who was at the scene of the emergency because he or a person he represents as an agent was soliciting business or seeking to perform a service for remuneration.

Similar Good Samaritan laws exist in many other states. Interveners should be familiar with the content of the law that applies to them.

Unless an intervener has a preexisting duty to intervene in another person's crisis, the law does not require that anyone intervene in the crisis of anyone else. Police, fire fighters, and emergency service personnel usually have a preexisting duty because they are hired to perform such tasks. Further, once an intervener has begun an intervention with another person, the intervention must continue unless the intervener is relieved by someone with greater competency. Not to do so could be construed as abandonment and could expose the intervener to legal consequences.

The courts generally determine liability, so all interveners should understand the concepts of negligence, or malpractice, for which the courts might hold interveners liable. In Crisis Intervention, good intentions are often not enough to avoid legal problems.

Negligence could result when an intervener assumes a duty of reasonable care for a victim and then breaches that duty, thereby causing damage or further injury to the victim. Generally, except when interveners have a preexisting duty, they are not required to intervene with a victim. Their moral or ethical values may dictate otherwise, however.

If an intervener, with or without a preexisting duty, decides to intervene with a sufferer, the intervener may assume a duty of reasonable care for that sufferer. Further, such a duty may be seen as assumed if the intervener acts in a way that creates a foreseeable risk to the victim.

For example, an intervener decides to take action to assist a sufferer. The action resulting from that decision creates a foreseeable risk to the victim; that is, the intervener's action could adversely affect the victim. In this case, the intervener has assumed a duty of reasonable care. If the usual procedure in this particular intervention is to remove the victim from the crisis situation, and the intervener decides against such movement, such a decision might cause additional injury to the victim.

If, as a result of such action, the victim is injured further or is damaged in other ways, the intervener may be said to have breached the duty of reasonable care and to have acted negligently. In such a case, a court might be asked to decide the intervener's liability based on the damages caused. Generally, the measure of negligence the court applies will be the standard of care given by the intervener. It must also be shown that the intervener's actions are the proximate or direct cause of the injury that the sufferer sustains.

Conversely, should the intervener decide not to intervene, lack of action would not create a duty of reasonable care because the intervener's actions—or inaction—would not have created risk to the victim other than that already experienced by the victim at that time. Even though inaction might allow the victim's suffering to continue, no duty of reasonable care has been created because in this case there is no duty to rescue. For police, fire fighters, and emergency medical service personnel, however, the exact opposite may be true because of their preexisting duty to act in such cases.

LEGAL GUIDELINES IN CRISIS INTERVENTION

The following guidelines are intended to help interveners avoid the difficulties of legal confrontations and to keep interveners where they belong, doing what they are best trained to do—serving in the field, helping victims manage the crises in their lives.

1. Always treat people as human beings, not just as cases.
2. Show respect to all with whom you are involved.
3. Intervene within the limits of your background and training. Do not exceed those limits, thereby committing the illegal practice of medicine, law, or psychology.
4. Unless you have a preexisting duty to intervene, consider carefully whether you want to perform an intervention.
5. Once you have begun to intervene, don't stop.
6. Discontinue your intervention only if you are relieved by someone with greater skill than your own.
7. Determine how the Good Samaritan laws relate to the types of intervention in which you may be involved.
8. If in doubt about your legal standing, contact a competent attorney and discuss your concerns.
9. Maintain confidentiality of all information you obtain about a crisis victim. Understand under what special circumstances you may have a duty to warn another person or to otherwise breach intervener-victim confidentiality.
10. Document everything you say and do with a victim. This may assist you later if you or your procedures are challenged.
11. Maintain your competency. Update your training and credentials as required.
12. Whenever possible, obtain the victim's consent before you assist with the crisis. If in doubt, ask!
13. If emergency circumstances do not allow for actual consent by the victim, you may be able to proceed under the concept of implied consent. In such circumstances, however, do only what is absolutely necessary to effectively intervene or rescue.

14. Do not disturb a crime scene. If you cannot avoid doing so, note exact locations of whatever is moved so that later you can give such information to proper authorities.
15. If you must search a victim's personal effects, try to have one or two witnesses present to observe your actions.
16. Know what you are required to report to the authorities. Requirements vary from state to state. (For example, child abuse must be reported in most states.)
17. Know the legal procedures in your jurisdiction for admissions for psychiatric care. Usually admissions are categorized as either voluntary or involuntary.
18. Remember that crisis interveners are not usually immune from observation of motor vehicle laws or from legal responsibility for vehicular accidents or property damage.
19. Respect the victim's right to privacy.
20. If the victim is a minor, obtain the permission of one of the parents before intervening. If this is not possible, you may be able to proceed under the doctrine of implied consent, as you would with an adult.
21. Be honest and open with victims.
22. Always think through what you will do, toward what end you will be doing it, what risks are present, and what safeguards you will apply.
23. Prepare yourself with knowledge of the law as well as of Crisis Intervention skills.
24. Remember that both acts of commission and acts of omission can affect liability.
25. Respect a sufferer's right to refuse your intervention.
26. Before entering a crisis victim's domain, dwelling, or office, request that person's permission. Know when the laws of your locality permit you to enter without permission.
27. If you are the director or supervisor of a Crisis Intervention agency, be sure all interveners and hot-line workers understand and can apply agency policies and procedures.
28. Within Crisis Intervention agencies, develop specific, understandable policies and procedures that clearly regulate and illustrate how intervention is to be performed.
29. As an agency director or supervisor, adhere to agency policy and insist that interveners do likewise.

30. Incorporate agency policies and legal issues into the training of crisis interveners.

LEGAL REFERENCES

The reader will find these references beneficial:

Arizona Revised Statute for Privileged Communications, § 32-2085 (1965). (Privileged Communications)

Buwa v. Smith, 84-1905 NMB (1986). (Duty to Warn)

Canterbury v. Spense, 464 F. 2d. 772 (D.C. Cir. 1972), cert. den. 93 S.Ct. 560 (1972). (Informed Consent)

Cutter v. Brownbridge, Cal. Ct. App., 1st Dist. 330 (1986). (Privileged Communications)

Hales v. Pittman, 118 Ariz. 305, 576 P. 2d. 493 (1978). (Informed Consent)

McDonald v. Clinger, 446 N.Y.S. 2d. 801 (1982). (Confidentiality)

McIntosb v. Milano, 403 A. 2d. 500 (N.J.S.Ct. 1979). (Duty to Warn)

New Jersey Revised Statutes, New Jersey Marriage Counseling Act, Annotated § 45: 8B-29 (1969). (Exceptions to Confidentiality)

People v. District Court, City and County of Denver, 719 P. 2d. 722 (Colo. 1986). (Privileged Communications)

Rodriguez v. Jackson, 118 Ariz. 13, 574 P. 2d. 481 (App. 1978). (Informed Consent)

Sard v. Hardy, 291 Md. 432, 379 A. 2d. 1014 (1977). (Informed Consent)

Tarasoff v. Regents of California, 131 Cal. Rptr. 14, 551 P. 2d. 334 (1976). (Duty to Warn)

Whitree v. State of New York, 56 Misc. 2d. 693, 290 N.Y.S. 2s. 486 (1968). (Record Keeping)

Appendix

THE AMERICAN BOARD OF EXAMINERS IN CRISIS INTERVENTION

The American College of Forensic Examiners (ACFE) is a not-for-profit, scientific and professional society. The recent alliance of ACFE and the American Board of Examiners in Crisis Intervention (ABECI) is welcomed by those of us who have labored for years to advance Crisis Intervention as a discipline of its own.

PURPOSE

The purpose of the ABECI is to provide a means of ensuring that individuals from various occupations and professions, and their potential or actual employers, have received extensive training in all aspects of emotional first aid and crisis management, and that they have adequately demonstrated their knowledge and ability in the effective means of Crisis Intervention. Further, the purpose of ABECI is to provide evaluation of individuals, regardless of previous professional levels of education, as to their levels of training and practical abilities to perform crisis intervention as mental health workers, psychologists, social workers, teachers, counselors, nurses, nonprofessional volunteers, law enforcement officers, firefighters, emergency medical response personnel, correctional officers, physicians, clergy, business executives, and union officials, among others. Sufficient evidence exists that it is these specialized skills, and not professional education alone, that ensure greater success in Crisis Intervention.

CERTIFICATION

The ABECI offers the opportunity for certification in the field of Crisis Intervention to those who demonstrate superior competence in the discipline. Generally, application to sit for the certification examination is submitted after completion of basic and advanced training courses in Crisis Intervention. These courses may be offered throughout the country by various training academies, regional chapters, and professional organizations and at national meetings, such as those sponsored by the American College of Forensic Examiners.

The certification examination is a day-long process that requires demonstrated skills. The testing consists of multiple forms of skill demonstrations covering significant general areas of Crisis Intervention. These areas are relevant to all occupations and professions providing emotional first aid. An applicant who successfully passes the certification examination is credentialed as a Certified Crisis Intervener (CCI).

DIPLOMATE STATUS

Diplomate status is for those professionals who can achieve the highest standards set forth by the ACFE/ABECI. Applicants must be members of ACFE and have a minimum of three years' experience in Crisis Intervention Services and/or significant related Crisis Intervention training. Also, candidates must have no record of disciplinary action from any state, province, or territory licensing or certification board during the last ten years. Appropriate point credit is given for the highest degree held and other major accomplishments in the field of Crisis Intervention. During the "grandfather/grandmother" period, an applicant attaining the required points will be credentialed as a Diplomate of the American Board of Examiners in Crisis Intervention (DABECI).

WEB ADDRESSES

ACFE: *www.acfe.com*
ABECI: *www.emotionalfirstaid.com*

Bibliography

APA & MTV (1999, October). Music Television 1999. *Warning Signs: A Violence Prevention Guide for Youth*. Washington, DC: Author.

Arizona Revised Statue for Priveleged Communciations, §32-2085 (1965).

Buwa v. Smith, 84-1905 NMB (1986).

Canterbury v. Spense, 464 F. 2d. 772 (D.C. Cir. 1972), cert. den. 93 S.Ct. 560 (1972).

Corsini, R. J. (1981). *Innovative Psychotherapies*. New York: Wiley Interscience.

Cutter v. Brownbridge, Cal. Ct. App., 1st Dist. (1986).

Evarts, W. R., Greenstone, J. L., Kirkpatrick, G., & Leviton, S. C. (1984) *Winning through accommodation: The mediator's handbook*. Dubuque, IA: Kendall/Hunt.

Fowler, W. R., & Greenstone, J.L. (1983). Hostage negotiations. In R. Corsini (Ed.), *Encyclopedia of psychology*. New York: Wiley.

Fowler, W. R., & Greenstone, J. L. (1987) Hostage negotiations for police. In R. Corsini (Ed.), *Concise encyclopedia of psychology*. New York: Wiley Interscience.

Fowler, W. R., & Greenstone, J. L. (1989). *Crisis intervention compendium*. Littleton, MA: Copley.

Greenstone, J. L. (1969) Tuning in with our children. *The Single Parent, 1,* 1–5.

Greenstone, J. L. (1970). *The meaning of psychology: A human subject*. Dubuque, IA: Kendall/Hunt.

Greenstone, J. L. (1971). The crisis of discipline. *The Single Parent, 2,* 5–10.

Greenstone, J. L. (1973). Parent's voice . . . child's voice. *The Single Parent, 2,* 5–8.

Greenstone, J. L. (1978). An interdisciplinary approach to marital disputes arbitration: The Dallas plan. *Conciliation Courts Review, 16,* 7–15.

Greenstone, J. L. (1981). Job related stress: Is it killing you? *National Law Journal, 4,* 30–34.

Greenstone, J. L. (1981, July). *Hostage survival*. Paper presented at the meeting of the Plano Amateur Radio Club, Dallas, TX.

Greenstone, J. L. (1981, October). *Crisis intervention: Stress and the police officer.* Paper presented at the meeting of the Society for Police and Criminal Psychology, Baton Rouge, LA.

Greenstone, J. L. (1982, November). *Crisis intervention and what to do if taken hostage.* Paper presented at the meeting of the Protestant Men's Club, Dallas, TX.

Greenstone, J. L. (1983, February 13). The divorce referee. *Dallas Morning News,* "Today" section, p. 20.

Greenstone, J. L. (1984). The crisis at Christmas. *Emotional First Aid: A Journal of Crisis Intervention, 1,* 21–29.

Greenstone, J. L. (1984, December 13). Holiday doesn't replace therapy: Crisis steps to avoid. *Northwest Passage,* pp. 1–2.

Greenstone, J. L. (1986, June). *Alternatives in dispute resolution: Family and marital mediation.* Paper presented at the meeting of the Fifth International Congress of Family Therapy, Jerusalem, Israel.

Greenstone, J. L. (1986). The laws of terrorism. *Emotional First Aid: A Journal of Crisis Intervention, 3,* 150–160.

Greenstone, J. L. (1992). The art of negotiating: Tactics and negotiating techniques—the way of the past and the way of the future. *Command: Journal of the Texas Tactical Police Officers Association, 1,* 11–18.

Greenstone, J. L. (1992). The key to success for hostage negotiations teams: Training, training and more training. *Police Forum, 1,* 3–4.

Greenstone, J. L. (1992, April). *Mediation advocacy: A new concept in the arena of family dispute resolution.* Paper presented at the meeting of the Sixth International Congress on Family Therapy: Divorce and Remarriage Interdisciplinary Issues and Approaches, Jerusalem, Israel.

Greenstone, J. L., & Leviton, S. C. (1979). *The crisis intervener's handbook, volume 1.* Dallas, TX: Crisis Management Workshops.

Greenstone, J. L., & Leviton, S. C. (1979). *Crisis management and intervener survival.* Tulsa, OK: Affective House.

Greenstone, J. L., & Leviton, S. C. (1979, July). *Intervention and emergency therapy in marriage and family crises.* Paper presented at the Third International Congress of Family Therapy and Family Life Education, Tel Aviv, Israel.

Greenstone, J. L., & Leviton, S. C. (1979). *Stress reduction: Personal energy management.* Tulsa, OK: Affective House.

Greenstone, J. L., & Leviton, S. C. (1980). *The crisis intervener's handbook, volume 2.* Dallas, TX: Rothschild.

Greenstone, J. L., & Leviton, S. C. (1980). Crisis management: A basic concern. *Crisis Intervener's Newsletter, 1,* 1–2.

Greenstone, J. L., & Leviton, S. C. (1981). Crisis management and intervener survival. In R. Corsini (Ed.), *Innovative psychotherapies.* New York: Wiley Interscience.

Greenstone, J. L., & Leviton, S. C. (1981) *Hotline: Crisis intervention directory.* New York: Facts on file.

Greenstone, J. L., & Leviton, S. C. (1981). *Training the trainer.* Tulsa, OK: Affective House.

Greenstone, J. L., & Leviton, S. C. (1982). *Crisis intervention: Handbook for interveners.* Dubuque, IA: Kendall/Hunt.

Greenstone, J. L., & Leviton, S. C. (1983). Crisis intervention. In R. Corsini (Ed.), *Encyclopedia of psychology.* New York: Wiley.

Greenstone, J. L., & Leviton, S. C. (1983, January). Divorce mediation. *D Magazine,* pp. 3–5.

Greenstone, J. L., & Leviton, S. C. (1983, March). *Divorce mediation and the attorney.* Paper presented at the meeting of the Family Law Section of the Dallas Bar Association, Dallas, TX.

Greenstone, J. L., & Leviton, S. C. (1983). Executive survival. In R. Corsini (Ed.), *Encyclopedia of psychology.* New York: Wiley.

Greenstone, J. L., & Leviton, S. C. (1983, March). *Mediation: An alternative to litigation.* Paper presented at the meeting of the Academy of Criminal Justice Sciences, San Antonio, TX.

Greenstone, J. L., & Leviton, S. C. (1983, July). *Mediation: Family dispute resolution.* Paper presented at the meeting of the Fourth International Congress of Family Therapy, Tel Aviv, Israel.

Greenstone, J. L., & Leviton, S. C. (1984, March). *Divorce mediation: The way of the 80's.* Paper presented at the meeting of the Oklahoma Association of Marriage and Family Therapists, Tulsa, OK.

Greenstone, J. L., & Leviton, S. C. (1984, September). *Crisis intervention in mediation.* Paper presented at the meeting of the National Conference on Peace and Conflict Resolution, St. Louis, MO.

Greenstone, J. L., & Leviton, S. C. (1984, September). *Management mediation: The police officer's alternative to litigation.* Paper presented at the meeting of the First National Symposium on Police Psychological Services, Quantico, VA.

Greenstone, J. L., & Leviton, S. C. (1984, December). *Crisis management for the mediator.* Paper presented at the meeting of the Second Annual Conference on Problem Solving through Mediation, Albany, NY.

Greenstone, J. L., & Leviton, S. C. (1986, July). *The dispute mediator as crisis manager: Crisis intervention skills for the mediator in high stress, high risk situations.* Paper presented at the meeting of the Academy of Family Mediators, Minneapolis, MN.

Greenstone, J. L., & Leviton, S. C. (1986). Intervention procedures. *Emotional First Aid: A Journal of Crisis Intervention, 3,* 100–110.

Greenstone, J. L., & Leviton, S. C. (1986). Mediation: The police officer's alternative to litigation. In *Psychological services for law enforcement.* Washington, D.C.: U.S. Department of Justice, Federal Bureau of Investigation, U.S. Government Printing Office.

Greenstone, J. L., & Leviton, S. C. (1986). Referrals: A key to successful crisis intervention. *Emotional First Aid: A Journal of Crisis Intervention, 3,* 75–80.

Greenstone, J. L., & Leviton, S. C. (1987). Crisis intervention. In R. Corsini (Ed.), *Concise encyclopedia of psychology.* New York: Wiley Interscience.

Greenstone, J. L., & Leviton, S. C. (1987, July). *Crisis intervention for mediators in high risk, high stress, potentially violent situations.* Paper presented at the meeting of the Academy of Family Mediators, New York.

Greenstone, J. L., & Leviton, S. C. (1987). Crisis management for mediators in high stress, high risk, potentially violent situations. *Mediation Quarterly, 3,* 20–30.

Greenstone, J. L., & Leviton, S. C. (1987). Executive survival. In R. Corsini (Ed.), *Concise Encyclopedia of Psychology.* New York: Wiley Interscience.

Greenstone, J. L., & Leviton, S. C. (1991). *Parents, kids, and war: Information designed to assist parents and children in handling war and its consequences.* Dallas: Leviton & Greenstone.

Greenstone, J. L., & Leviton, S. C. (1992, April). *Crisis management for mediators in high stress, high risk, potentially violent family and divorce mediations.* Paper presented at the meeting of the Sixth International Congress on Family Therapy: Divorce and Remarriage Interdisciplinary Issues and Approaches, Jerusalem, Israel.

Greenstone, J. L., & Rosenbluh, E. S. (1980). Evolution of the American Academy of Crisis Interveners and the Southwestern Academy of Crisis Interveners. *Crisis Intervener's Newsletter, 1,* 13–14.

Hales v. Pittman, 118 Ariz. 305, 576 P. 2d. 493 (1978).

Hendricks, J., & Greenstone, J. L. (1982, March). *Crisis intervention in criminal justice.* Paper presented at the meeting of the Academy of Criminal Justice Sciences, Louisville, KY.

Holmes, T. H., U Rahe, R. H. (1967). The social readjustment rating scale. *Journal of Psychosomatic Research, 11,* 213–218.

Holmes, T. H., & Masuda, M. (1973). Life change and illness susceptibility. In B. S. Dohrenwend U B. P. Dohrenwend (Eds.), *Stressful life events: Their nature and effects.* New York: Wiley.

Is your kid a killer? (1999). *Psychology Today, 32,* 16.

Lerner, M. D. (1999). Identifying students "At-Risk" for Violent Behavior: A Checklist of "Early Warning Signs." *A Practical Guide for Crisis Response in Our Schools,* p. 38. (Available from the American Academy of Experts in Traumatic Stress, 368 Veterans Memorial Highway, Commack, New York 11725.

Leviton, S. C. (1982). National Institute for Crisis Intervention lecture, Louisville, KY.

Leviton, S. C., & Greenstone, J. L. (1980). Intervener survival: Dealing with the givens. *Emotional First Aid: A Journal of Crisis Intervention, 2,* 15–20.

Leviton, S. C., & Greenstone, J. L. (1983). Conflict mediation. In R. Corsini (Ed.), *Encyclopedia of psychology.* New York: Wiley.

Leviton, S. C., & Greenstone, J. L. (1983). Intervener survival. In R. Corsini (Ed.), *Encyclopedia of psychology.* New York: Wiley.

Leviton, S. C., & Greenstone, J. L. (1984). Mediation in potential crisis situations. *Emotional First Aid: A Journal of Crisis Intervention, 1,* 150–155.

Leviton, S. C., & Greenstone, J. L. (1984). Team intervention. *Emotional First Aid: A Journal of Crisis Intervention, 1,* 20–25.

Leviton, S. C., & Greenstone, J. L. (1987). Conflict mediation. In R. Corsini (Ed.), *Concise encyclopedia of psychology.* New York: Wiley Interscience.

Leviton, S. C., & Greenstone, J. L. (1987). Intervener survival. In R. Corsini (Ed.), *Concise encyclopedia of psychology.* New York: Wiley Interscience.

Leviton, S. C., & Greenstone, J. L. (1997). *Elements of Mediation.* Pacific Grove, CA: Brooks/Cole.

McDonald v. Clinger, 446 N.Y.S. 2d. 801 (1982).

McIntosh v. Milano, 403 A. 2d. 500 (N.J.S.Ct. 1979)

Mitchell, J. T., & Resnik, H. L. P. (1981). *Emergency response to crisis.* Bowie, MD: Brady.

Mitchell, J. T., (1983). When disaster strikes . . . the critical incident stress debriefing process. *Journal of Emergency Medical Services,* 8 (1), 36–39.

Mitchell, J. T., & Everly, G. S. (1996). *Critical incident stress debriefing: An operations manual.* Ellicott City, MD: Chevron Publishing Corp.

Mordock, J. B., Ellis, M. H., & Greenstone, J. L. (1969). The effects of group and individual therapy on sociometric choice of disturbed adolescents. *International Journal of Group Psychotherapy, 4,* 200–210.

New Jersey Revised Statutes, New Jersey Marriage Counseling Act, Annotated § 45: 8B-29 (1969). (Exceptions to Confidentiality)

Pederson, P. A. (1988). *A handbook for developing multicultural awareness.* New York: American Association for Counseling and Development.

People v. District Court, City and County of Denver, 719 P. 2d. 722 (Colo. 1986).

Rodriguez v. Jackson, 118 Ariz. 13, 574 P. 2d. 481 (App. 1978).

Rosenbluh, E. S. (1975). National Institute for Crisis Intervention lecture, Louisville, KY.

Rosenbluh, E. S. (1981). *Emotional first aid.* Louisville, KY: American Academy of Crisis Interveners.

Rosenbluh, E. S. (1986). *Crisis counseling: Emotional first aid.* Dubuque, IA: Kendall/Hunt.

Sard v. Hardy, 291 Md. 432, 379 A. 2d. 1014 (1977).

Selye, H. (1974). *Stress without distress.* Philadelphia: Lippencott.

Slaikeu, K. A. (1984). *Crisis intervention: A handbook for practice and research.* Boston: Allyn & Bacon.

Tarasoff v. Regents of California, 131 Cal. Rptr. 14, 551 P. 2d. 334 (1976).

Whitree v. State of New York, 56 Misc. 2d. 693, 290 N.Y.S. 2s 486 (1968).

TO THE OWNER OF THIS BOOK:

We hope that you have found *Elements of Crisis Intervention*, Second Edition, useful. So that this book can be improved in a future edition, would you take the time to complete this sheet and return it? Thank you.

School and address: _____

Department: _____

Instructor's name: _____

1. What I like most about this book is: _____

_____

_____

2. What I like least about this book is: _____

_____

_____

3. My general reaction to this book is: _____

_____

4. The name of the course in which I used this book is: _____

_____

5. Were all of the chapters of the book assigned for you to read? _____

   If not, which ones weren't? _____

6. In the space below, or on a separate sheet of paper, please write specific suggestions for
   ͘re about your experience in using the

   _____

   _____

   _____

   _____

   _____

Optional:

Your name: _____ Date: _____

May Brooks/Cole quote you, either in promotion for *Elements of Crisis Intervention,*
Second Edition, or in future publishing ventures?

Yes: _____ No: _____

Sincerely,

James L. Greenstone
Sharon C. Leviton

FOLD HERE

- -

- -

FOLD HERE